中国国家汉办赠送
Donated by Hanban, China

Cultural China Series

Fu Jin

CHINESE THEATER

Happiness and Sorrows on the Stage

Translated by Wang Wenliang, Wang Huan & Zhang Lina

CHINA
INTERCONTINENTAL
PRESS

图书在版编目（CIP）数据

中国戏剧：英文/傅谨著；王文亮，王欢，张丽娜译．—北京：五洲传播出版社，2010.1
ISBN 978-7-5085-1683-7

Ⅰ.①中… Ⅱ.①傅… ②王… ③王… ④张…Ⅲ.①戏剧史-中国-英文 Ⅳ.① J809.2
中国版本图书馆CIP数据核字（2009）第191274号

CHINESE THEATER

Happiness and Sorrows on the Stage

Author: Fu Jin

Translator: Wang Wenliang, Wang Huan & Zhang Lina

Executive Editor: Su Qian

Art Designer: Tang Ni

Publisher: China Intercontinental Press (6 Beixiaomachang, Lianhuachi Donglu, Haidian District, Beijing 100038, China)

Tel: 86-10-58891281

Website: www.cicc.org.cn

Printer: C&C Joint Printing Co., (Beijing) Ltd.

Format: 720×965mm 1/16

Edition: Jan. 2010, 1st edition, 1st print run

Price: RMB 94.00 (*yuan*)

Contents

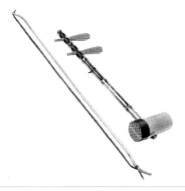

Foreword

China is a country with multiple theatrical activities spread over its vast area. Currently, Chinese traditional opera (*xiqu*), an integration of singing and performance, is the most common, unique and representative form of Chinese theater.

Chinese traditional opera originated in the 12th century. Compared with ancient Greek and Indian Sanskrit drama, it was born rather late but with more exuberant vitality. Over more than 800 years, Chinese

At the backstage, theatrical actors are busy making up for a splendid show.

traditional opera has maintained its basic form, therefore, among the existing types of drama, Chinese traditional opera may have the longest history.

Rich in history and charm in artistic expression, traditional opera is deeply loved by ancient Chinese people. A formula is extensively used in Chinese traditional opera performances, with a special music metric and regulated singing. The speaking of dramatic characters requires compliance with the rhythm of the poetry and in military opera, pattern of martial arts is used to demonstrate fighting scene.

Singing, speaking, acting and acrobatic fighting are four basic types of performance measures in Chinese traditional opera. These types of performance are based on the virtual principle. (Going upstairs, for example, in which the actors make physical response by lifting clothes and legs, switching across windows and doors, even though there are no real doors and windows on the stage. Another example, snapping a whip means riding a horse while paddling means sailing.) On the basis of realistic deformation and refinement, every move the actors make on stage, a smile or even a frown, can be rich in meaning, with a strong narrative nature, vividly reflecting the inner emotions of the character.

Extensive use of music reinforces the lyrical feature of the theater, which gives a special advantage to the Chinese traditional opera in dealing with the delicate psychological activity in complex situations facing the characters. In the overall structure, the main characters are commonly assigned to most singing work, especially in the core scenes, where changes in rhythm and emotion leave the

Ancient Peking Opera Garden.

deepest impression on the audience. Excellent actors are often quite popular for their singing ability and their unique means of expression and strong voices. Different theatrical genres are, therefore, formed according to the actors' characteristic vocal expressions and stage performance.

Based on the aesthetic principles of traditional Chinese theatrical performances, the theater stage has a high degree of virtualization. In addition to a simple

Love story of wits and beauties is the everlasting theme on the theatrical stage.

table, two chairs and a few essential props, the story takes place through a virtual performance, monologue and dialogue. That's why theatrical performances are flexible and can move and change freely. For example, actors sometimes move in a circle, which can represent traveling around mountains and waters.

Chinese traditional opera has definite rules of dress. Historical figures' theatrical clothing from the Ming Dynasty (1368–1644) has been transformed and beautified and is, as a general practice, used by almost every actor.

Make-up is often intense in color. Some male characters in particular have a fixed mask, which is exaggerated and uniquely shaped and often has a specific implication. A red-faced mask means justice, a black signifies bluntness, while white symbolizes treachery.

Singing, speaking, acting and acrobatic fighting are the four basic techniques of expression, but theaters in different parts of China fall under different genres. Theaters are categorized, first and foremost, by differences in melody, notes and musical instruments. These differences are related to local language. Across China's vast territory, people use sharply different language. For this reason, lyrical and narrative intentions can only be realized by the use of dialects the audience can understand. At the same time, the use of dialects can affect the style of the melody. There were once 300 different theater genres in China with about 200 still circulating, showing China's extremely rich and diverse theatrical styles.

From the beginning of the 20th century, subject to the impact of the West, the modern drama or stage play without singing appeared in China. For more than 100 years, modern drama has been gradually integrating into Chinese culture, taken root and become very influential. The development and prosperity of modern drama has added a new landscape for Chinese theater, which, as a whole, has become more diversified.

The traditional Chinese opera can be roughly divided into the sing plays and the military plays. The former one is based mainly on singing, speaking and acting, while the latter one is acrobatic fighting, which is quite popular among children.

Prelude: the Origins of Chinese Theater

Sacrifice and Entertainer

The origins of Chinese theater can be traced back 2,500 years. At the beginning stage of civilization, witches in tribal and ethnic groups held considerable power. Sacrificial ritual music and dance performances based on certain norms were special ways for witches to communicate with the gods. They were the channel between Heaven and Man, unifying the human world and the seemingly elusive spiritual world on which people could rely. The original theatrical art is closely related to the rich and varied sacrificial ceremonies.

As with the various cultures around the world, the prototype of Chinese theater appeared almost simultaneously with its civilization. However, mature theater was born much later. Mature theater didn't emerge until the 10th century, thousands of years later than that in ancient Greece, ancient India and other cultural centers.

Bronze chime bells of the Warring States Period, the main musical instruments in the sacrificial ceremony held by the imperial family and noblemen.

Early theater activities in ancient China were varied and interesting. In the embryonic stage of Chinese theater, singing was accompanied with dance; people dressed as animals and danced with a specific pace in the accompaniment of rhythmic music. These performances, often with connotative meaning, intended to tell some stories.

In *The Book of Songs*, completed in the Spring and Autumn Period (770–476 BC), China's earliest collection of poetry, a large number

The musical tower of the Town God's temple of the Tang Dynasty, a place for drama performance and sacrifice offering.

of poems, especially those based on folk songs were performed by singing and dancing with some emotional content displaying a trinity of literature, music and dance. The sacrificial ritual in the southern state of Chu during the Warring States Period (475–256 BC) also provided us with broad space for the imagination. The famous poet Qu Yuan (340–278 BC) during the Chu Period left a considerable amount of related poems, among which, *Nine Songs* and *Nine Chapters*, in particular, expressed his personal thoughts and served as a script for Chu's sacrificial ceremonies.

National Martyr in *Nine Songs* described the memorial ceremony for the national martyrs, which was better after theatrical components included in the ritual ceremonies. A large number of Chu songs circulating in southern China reflected that the early Chu had set a basic pattern for these large-scale sacrificial ceremonies. Through these poems, we see ancient people in the sacrificial ceremony where they sang a story poem and danced a non-abstract dance with theatrical action.

These ceremonies were not the actual theater in classic sense, but already had all the elements needed for a play.

At this period, in the court of vassal states, there were many entertainers aimed at pleasing the princes and aristocrats with comic performances. Their performances were also embryonic forms of theater.

The Spectacular Scene of Music and Dance

The Han Dynasty (202 BC–AD 220) witnessed a more rapid social development. During this period, various embryonic theater activities in both court and civil society entered a new phase.

Usually, Chinese ancient people prayed in spring and offered thanks of the harvest in autumn. That's why sacrificial activities with singing and dancing in spring and autumn were indispensable rituals for both court and people. What's more, the royal ceremony had already been highly systematized. In the meantime, the Han gradually developed an entertainment industry in towns and rural areas and developed some entertainment-oriented performances with folk artists living on acting. The court held large performances for the general public, which, to a certain extent, stimulated the private entertainment industry and allowed for a transfer of the center of entertainment performances from the court to the public. Together with frequent trade exchanges between China and Western countries, singing, dancing and acrobatics in Western Regions spread to Chang'an (present-day Xi'an). As a result, this political center of the Han became a meeting point and global center of multi-cultural entertainment performances.

The figurine of entertainer of the Han Dynasty depicts a comedian image.

During the Han Dynasty, many kinds of plays prevailed, including a variety of music and dance, acrobatics,

Theatrical characters in brick carving of the Han Dynasty.

and etc. A variety of performances from this era, including dancing and acrobatics, were closely related to the theater.

After the Han Dynasty, the development of music and dance was spectacular. The folk song and dance performance, *ta-yao-niang* first appeared during the Northern Qi Dynasty (550–577) and developed during the Tang Dynasty (618–907). *Ta-yao-niang* described family grudges. Its protagonist, a woman often bullied at home by her drunken husband told passers-by over and over about her miserable life, while her ugly husband beat his grieved wife in public. The story was accompanied by her singing and dancing. These two actors performed as a future song-and-dance duet (*er ren zhuan*), with a female lead and a jester. The female lead acted through song, dance and speech.

From the Han to the Tang Dynasty, song and dance forms like *ta-yao-niang, su-mu-zhe, lan-ling-wang* and *bo-tou* gradually took shape, meaning China entered a new era of entertainment culture. During the Sui (581–618) and Tang dynasties, the development of ancient Chinese music and dance reached a summit. In Dunhuang, you can see countless murals left from that time, reproducing the busy and flourishing life of

Song-and-dance duet (er ren zhuan)
Song-and-dance duet (*er ren zhuan*) is a popular folk art prevalent in Liaoning, Jilin, Heilongjiang provinces and eastern Inner Mongolia. It enjoyed nearly 300 years of history after its creation. Its typical expression is a man and a woman with bright clothes, fans and handkerchiefs dancing and singing high-pitched rough songs with witty humorous lyrics.

The Dunhuang mural painting artistically expresses the spectacular scene of music and dance of the Tang Dynasty.

The painting of *Musical Scene in Palace* depicts the scene where the maids in palace of the Tang Dynasty are enjoying a feast and playing music.

the era.

Xinong and the Art of Singing with Speaking

Funny and humorous performances can be traced back to the pre-Qin period, when entertainers in court made fun called *xinong*.

The *canjun* opera showed that the development of Chinese theater was close to maturity. The *canjun* opera was used to tease and had two roles. The teased was called *canjun* and the teaser was *canghu*. Until the late Tang Dynasty, *canjun* opera evolved to include more performers and a more complex dramatic plot with twists and turns.

From the dramatic point of view, the main purpose of the *canjun* opera was to poke fun but it had roles, stories and plots. It was an embryonic form of theater. Based on dialogue and humorous performances, *canjun* opera, along with performances such as *ta-yao-niang* constituted two basic forms of Chinese theater.

The mural painting of music and dance in a tomb of the Song Dynasty in Henan Province.

The painting of *Children Watching Acrobatic Show* of the Song Dynasty. In the picture, the acrobatic performer sings and beats the drum at the same time, attracting two children.

Canjun opera had a direct impact on the creation of *zaju* during the Song (960–1279) and Jin (1115–1234) dynasties. *Canjun* opera, as with entertainers' performances in early periods, was mostly improvised and allowed for the creation of new jokes on the spot. These occasional impromptu performances gradually became fixed programs, frequently staged during the Tang, Song and Jin dynasties.

Xinong, similar to *canjun* opera, developed quickly. These were the early form of Song Jin *zaju*. Such comic theater, mostly simple and short, in addition to jest-based burlesque, contained a number of miscellaneous play rap. Song Jin *zaju* accumulated a great deal of material, and after the emergence of mature theater, its short yet sturdy forms were inserted into modern theater and became an integral part.

During the Tang and Song dynasties, sizeable cities such as Chang'an, Kaifeng and Hangzhou had prosperous economies and large populations that promoted the development of entertainment industries of considerable scale. A variety of performance-oriented entertainment and arts industries converged. Fierce market competition put tremendous pressure on the operation of theater, prompting people to continue to enhance the standard of performance.

In the Tang and Song dynasties, interpreting history was very popular and was considered as the first long narrative literature in Chinese history. The stories were created when these storytellers performed in public, then became more and more complex with many twists and turns on the way to become large-scale dramatic works.

Buddhism was also a catalyst in the emergence and prosperity of story-telling theater. It was introduced to China during the Eastern Han Dynasty (25–220) and expanded its influence afterwards. The

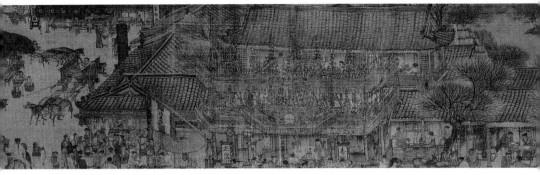

Scroll of Along the River During the Qingming Festival (Part), by Zhang Zeduan of the Song Dynasty. It is a vivid description of the bustling and hustling capital city, Bianliang in the Northern Song Dynasty, with a theatre next to the street in the left of the picture.

Tang Dynasty saw the extensive spread of Buddhism. In temples, there were Suttantikas and Buddhist chanters, leading the monks to read sutra and expound the texts in vulgar ways to propagate Buddhism. The monks compiled scripture and moving stories into popular text, which was interpreted in prose at the beginning and then rendered into singing verse. As a result, a special style called *bianwen* emerged.

To meet the changing interests of the audience, the monks speaking and singing *bianwen* were allowed to preach based on a story that may have even been irrelevant to the scripture and doctrine of Buddhism. The temporal speech then evolved into a special kind of mass entertainment.

From *bianwen* style, we can find the origins of story-telling theater in the Tang and Song dynasties. Their scripts bore some resemblance in style but the latter was more similar to *zhu gongdiao*, which was related to *bianwen*.

Zhu Gongdiao of Romance of the West Bower (*Xi Xiang Ji Zhu Gongdiao*) created by Dong Jieyuan was the most complete work of zhu *gongdiao* of its time. It later evolved into the famous classic theater *Romance of the West Bower* (*Xi Xiang Ji*), and created the most classic story mode in the history of Chinese theater. In the story, a young man meets a beauty on his road to the

The silk painting of Song *zaju*, in which two actresses play the male roles. The dramatic form that actresses exclusively play male roles is popular in the Song Dynasty.

The brick carving of Jin *zaju* at a tomb in Jishan, Shanxi province vividly describes the shape and expression of *zaju* characters.

Gongdiao

Gongdiao is a term used in ancient Chinese theater that refers to various musical modes, which then sets a dramatic tune. The order of twelve temperaments with seven tunes, including *gong, shang, jiao, zhi, yu, biangong* and *bianzhi* was the basic order followed in all dynasties. The musical mode dominated by the *gong* temperament is called *gong*, otherwise, it was diao. Seven tunes accompanied by twelve temperaments could obtain twelve *gong* and seventy-two *diao*, forging eighty-four *gongdiao*.

imperial examination. They fall in love at first glance and are secretly engaged, but then separate under family pressure. When the man comes first in the final imperial examination, he wins back his lover. Meeting, loving, parting and reunion completed a dramatic process.

A strong desire for love in adolescence was always the main driving force of dramatic development, ranging from sweet love, pain and longing after separation, to the joy of reunion. The richness of emotion ensured a moving content for the story. *Zhu Gongdiao of Romance of the West Bower* included fourteen different *gongdiao* and about 150 basic melodies.

During the Sui and Tang dynasties many large-scale musical works emerged. They were made up of different tunes in the same *gongdiao*. However, when the description of complete and complex story was concerned, their pattern was not enough. Also taking into account the way in which the complicated story was expressed by music, a more varied musical means was needed. In the formation of *zhu gongdiao*, Tang and Song tunes and folk music common in ci poetry of the Song all were utilized, which in turn, livened up the *zhu gongdiao*.

Peaks Towering Magnificently:
Song *Xiwen* and Yuan *Zaju*

Southern *Xiwen* during the Song Dynasty

Emerging during the Song Dynasty, the earliest mature theater in China flourished in Zhejiang and was called Wenzhou *zaju*. It was sharply different from Song Jin *zaju* in two ways. On the one hand, actors in Song Jin *zaju* didn't necessarily play fixed roles whose main purpose was to make fun. On the other, it was a small-sized xinong without complete stories.

During the late Southern Song Dynasty (1127–1279), new theater emerged with set length and complete stories in which actors played dramatic roles and performed by various means including speech and song. Moreover, such performances maintained their basic forms to the present day. The highly sophisticated theater style during the Southern Song Dynasty emerged in Wenzhou and flourished in southern area of the Yangtze River and was known as "southern tune *xiwen*" or simply referred to as "*xiwen*."

The earliest complete script was found and repurchased in 1920 in a small antique shop in London by scholar Ye Gongchuo. It included works such as *The No.1 Scholar Zhang Xie* (*Zhang Xie Zhuang Yuan*), *The Butcher* (*Xiao Sun Tu*) and *Wrong Career of Official's Son* (*Huan Men Zi Di Cuo Li Shen*).

The No.1 Scholar Zhang Xie was compiled by the scholars in the Jiushan Club in Wenzhou during the Southern Song Dynasty. During this period, *xiwen* performances were very popular in Wenzhou and literary societies were common. The Jiushan Club, a professional group for script writing, was also founded. The club was very active. For instance, when a monk named Zu Jie in Wenzhou did all kinds of evil things under the asylum of local officials, the club members immediately compiled a *xiwen* script based on the monks' misdemeanors and performed it in public. The theater then aroused the anger of the local population, forcing the government to uphold justice and punish the evil monk. The script did not survive but, to some extent, the play demonstrated the existence and role of theater in society.

Wenzhou was not a central city and members of the Jiushan Club were merely scholars good at script writing. During the Song and Yuan dynasties, these scholars from the middle and lower class of the society had close relationships with artists. They were well-trained on poetry writing as early as childhood, had a regular contact with popular music and dance artists and were able to skillfully master script writing skills. They laid a literary foundation for Chinese folk theater as was the case with *The No.1 Scholar Zhang Xie* and other early plays, which were mature enough to stage as large-scale dramatic performances.

The No.1 Scholar Zhang Xie was mainly about a bookman Zhang Xie. On his way to the imperial examination, Zhang encounters bandits in Wuji Mountain. Seriously wounded and badly looted, he flees to a nearby temple. In a blissful encounter in the temple, he meets a poor maiden who earns a living by weaving cotton cloth and comes to her aid. The two then are married and vow to spend their remaining years together. Two months after their marriage,

Stage photo of Peking Opera *The No.1 Scholar Zhang Xie*.

Zhang recovers and intends to go to Beijing to take exams. Since he is penniless and cannot afford the long journey, his wife sold her hair to cover Zhang's traveling expenses. Zhang Xie goes to the capital and successfully comes first in the examination. Zhang is proud of his success. He refuses the love of another woman, Wang Jinhua, the daughter of Prime Minister Wang Deyong. Struck down, Wang Jinhua grieves to death. But Zhang's refusal was not due to his deep love for his wife. The poor woman had followed Zhang to Beijing after learning of Zhang's success. He, on the contrary, suspects the poor woman, looks down upon her for her humble birth and then drives her out of the official building. Later, Zhang is assigned an office out of Beijing. En route, he passes through Wuji Mountain and meets his wife, who begged all the way back home. Zhang tries to kill her with his sword and she is seriously injured falling off a cliff. At the same time, the Prime Minister Wang Deyong requests to act as Zhang's direct supervisor after the death of his daughter. On his way to take office, he saves the poor wounded woman and adopts her as a daughter. Zhang is deeply regretted for offending Wang and now seeks to marry his daughter with the help of a matchmaker. In the bridal chamber, Zhang recognizes the woman he abandoned and is extremely shamed. The woman also refuses to marry the man. At last, persuaded by Wang, the two bury the hatchet and are reunited again.

The No.1 Scholar Zhang Xie was an attractive story with winding and complicated plots. The play's emotion was focused on poor weak women, while officials of high rank were outrageously criticized. It clearly highlighted the author's moral evaluation, representing a certain aesthetic taste of the era.

Xiwen spread widely in the Southern Song Dynasty, the earliest works among which were *Chaste Woman Zhao and Cai Erlang* (*Zhao Zhen Nü Cai Er Lang*) and *Wang Kui Betrays Gui-Ying* (*Wang Kui Fu Gui Ying*), according to literature records. Their themes were similar to *The No.1 Scholar Zhang Xie* which was about men's rise to

Dramatic roles fall into five categories, namely, *sheng* (*a male lead*), *dan* (*a female lead*), *jing* (*a supporting male lead*), *chou* (*the jester*) and *mo* (*a male role*), which can be further divided according to gender, age and characteristics. The photo shows a *laosheng* (*an old male lead*) and *huadan* (*a young female lead*).

fortune and then betrayal to their original love. In these stories, the social status of the hero and heroine is clear and the authors always stand on the side of the poor and disadvantaged women. These works of folklore were welcomed by the ordinary people, not only because of their dedicated artistic means of expression but also because of their audacity to reward virtue and punish vice.

The occurrence of *xiwen* during the Song Dynasty represented by *The No.1 Scholar Zhang Xie* was a miracle. The Song was repeatedly defeated in the war fought with Liao (907–1125) and Jin until the Song migrated to the South and the Jin took the North. As a result, a 150-year-long division of North and South was formed. The capital of Southern Song Dynasty was located in Lin'an (present-day Hangzhou) whose entertainment industry was greatly stimulated by the development of theater.

Besides, the office in charge of music in the court alternated between founding and abolishing theater projects, so that a large group of artistic talents originally gathered in the court and trained systematically began to flood to society, resulting in the enhancement of overall performance levels and the intensification of market competition. All these factors pointed to a more attractive and ornamental style of performance. *Xiwen* was an exact product. However, what is surprising was that once it was born, it already possessed all the elements required for a mature theater, like an artistic peak towering out of a flat land.

The No.1 Scholar Zhang Xie was not merely a form of combined speech and song but a full-fledged theater. It was a typical prosopopeia in genre and narrative method, providing an essential condition to mature theater. It also possessed a complete music structure with southern tune as its main body, blazing a brilliant road to Chinese theater.

It was true that *xiwen* including *The No.1 Scholar Zhang Xie* was closely related to the art of singing with speaking in the Tang and Song dynasties. Dozens of theater scripts, whose themes and story framework, as well as their main characters were repeated countless times by artists on the stage and were well known to the audience. After transformation and refinement, they quickly evolved into theaters. Their development track was clearly visible.

Xiwen, *bianwen* and *zhu gongdiao* bore a clear relationship of inheritance. However, they had differences that lay in their genre. While *bianwen* and *zhu gongdiao* were narratives, *xiwen* was prosopopeia. The genre disparity differentiated theater from the art of singing and speaking. In the latter form, there were one or two narrators conveying the message of others by using the third person, instead of being the characters in the story. On the contrary, actors in theater pretended to play roles of characters in the story and used the first person to sing and speak. With the same story framework and the same characters, but differentiated in means of expression, the art of singing and speaking and theater were clearly distinct.

However, what was more interesting was that in the script of *The No.1 Scholar Zhang Xie*, we can find some tracks left by the evolution from *zhu gongdiao* into *xiwen*. The opening scenes were similar to *zhu gongdiao*. An actor performed in the style of *zhu gongdiao* and urged the audience to be quiet for a moment and stop laughing. He then interpreted how the script came into being, adapted from the original *zhu gongdiao* work *The Biography of Zhang Xie* (*Zhang Xie Zhuang Yuan Zhuan*). The purpose of the adaptation was to win a competition and change the genre of the performance. It was then followed by performances by many actors playing different roles. As a result, the transformation from narrative to prosopopeia or from the art of singing and speaking to theater was complete. In an era when the audience was accustomed to narrative, theater was still quite ready to emerge. Therefore, it was a matter of course that much necessary groundwork had to be done before a grand show.

In *xiwen*, actors played dramatic characters. From the Southern Song, Chinese theater began to adopt a typical role-playing system.

In *The No.1 Scholar Zhang Xie*, *sheng* (a male lead), *dan* (a female lead), *jing* (a supporting male lead), *chou* (the jester) and *mo* (a male role) were all in place, and sometimes, would be supplemented by *wai* (a spare role), when the main roles had to be played by more than one person at the same time. In *The No.1 Scholar Zhang Xie*, a *sheng* played the role of Zhang, while the poor maiden was played by the *dan*. However, an actor was not confined to one dramatic character; on the contrary, he was free to take the role of two or three characters, as long as there was no need for these characters to be on stage at one time. In the above theater, *mo, jing* and *chou* all appear frequently, taking part in multiple scenes.

The typical system of role-play in Chinese theater could find its full expression in the theater script. In most occasions, *jing* and *chou* were responsible for fun parts, considered as descendents of *canjun* and *canghu* in the era of *canjun* opera. *Mo* played an even more crucial role as a guide, who, from time to time, jumped out of the theater to introduce the event, make some comments and glamorize the atmosphere. He was also able to play the role of

Role-play system

The role-play system was an important and special system in Chinese traditional opera, related to the formation of theatrical troupes and the division of actors. It originated from *canjun* opera, in which only two actors had performances. As the number of characters in Song Jin *zaju* increased, artists began to duly assume their respective duties. The system in which different artists impersonate different types of dramatic characters was referred to as "role-play." From the original theatrical troupes, actors, without exception performed fixed roles such as *sheng, dan, jing, chou,* or *mo.* Plots became more complex, however, and it often occurred that when two or even more dramatic characters of the same type had to be on stage at the same time, the theatrical troupe had to be enlarged. However, actors of the same type of roles were in an unequal status. For example, when two *dan* were needed in one theater, such as a mistress and a maiden servant, the much more important role, namely a mistress was played by *dan,* and the lesser one by *tie dan.*

narrator.

From the Song Dynasty onwards, when actors performed on stage, roles rather than characters in the theater were specified, for instance, *sheng* or *dan* was marked instead of Zhang Xie or the poor maiden; and it was no exception when one actor played the role of more than one character, since he could introduce himself or be introduced so as to be known. That's why the script of Chinese theater served as a clue for actors to play on the stage, rather than a text for reading.

Take an example of the role-play system. The script was not supposed to be read by the audience since it did not really provide information about the event or the destiny of the characters. Instead, it offered tips for actors about who was the next to go on stage, what should he sing or speak on stage and how he could act.

The No.1 Scholar Zhang Xie was endowed with the typical stage art form in Chinese theater, that is, the scene where the dramatic event occurred was revealed by a virtual performance. Here is a typical example. When Zhang was seriously injured by the bandits in Wuji Mountain and escaped to the nearby temple, the dramatic setting was changed into *jing, mo* and *chou,* playing respectively the role of Mountain God, the judge and the clown. When Zhang entered the temple, *jing* ordered *mo* and *chou* to change into two temple doors. As he pushed the door, what he pushed was actually *mo* and *chou.* Since Zhang was badly wounded, he had to lean against the door when it was closed, and leaned on *chou.* Later, when the poor maiden returned to the temple, she had to knock at the door which was cushioned by Zhang, and chou,

A male *chou* and a female *chou*.

impersonating the door, made the sound as a knock on the door. When the poor maiden made the movement of knocking, *chou* even said, "you could also knock on the other door." On the wedding day, *mo* takes the role of Uncle Li, while *jing* is Aunt Li, and *chou* the waiter. However, at the wedding reception, *chou*, the former waiter, bows to one knee and braces himself to the ground with two hands, serving as a table for dinner. When Zhang Xie, the poor maiden, Uncle Zhang, and Aunt Li drink the wine, the table begins to sing: "I bow from the waist to serve you, so may you be kind to offer with me some wine drink?"

Such performances, to be sure, teased the audience but also demonstrated a typical stage pattern of Chinese theater. The virtual performance on the stage, or a typical mean where complicated stage props were replaced by performances, was born during the Song Dynasty and lasts to the present day.

From the 20th century, Chinese theatrical scholars reached a consensus on referring to the typical theatrical form which contained full stories, facing the audience to act by using multiple vehicles including singing, dancing and speaking as *xiqu*.

With the emergence of *xiwen*, Chinese theater successfully evolved into a pattern. If *xiqu* is considered as representative of Chinese theater, then, all those simple and primitive plays of the past thousand years serve as its foreshadow. During the Ming

(1368–1644) and Qing (1616–1911) dynasties, artists were used to calling the small-sized *xinong* and musical dance "small opera," differentiating them from large-scale "big opera."

The Prosperity of Yuan *Zaju*

In the 13th century, the Mongols destroyed the Southern Song Dynasty, and established a unified Yuan Dynasty. After that, Mongols ruled the Han people, especially those in the south with an iron hand. But even so, Yuan witnessed the most important development in Chinese theater history.

During the Yuan Dynasty, *zaju* was prevalent, especially during the most prosperous cities such as Kaifeng, Luoyang and Lin'an.

A systematic official prostitute system was born during the Song and Tang dynasties, when the singing girls were responsible for amusing officials at the command of the court or local government, and were permitted to put on some commercial performances. During the Yuan Dynasty, *zaju* became the mainstream dramatic form and was played by the prestigious singing girls. Affected by the singing girls, artist groups engaged in traveling entertainment show appeared.

Zaju then spread throughout the country, and even into rural areas. The Yuan Dynasty left a good number of classic *zaju* works and was a peak in the history of Chinese literature, whose literary value was no less than that of any time in history. Many talented scholars didn't involve in politics because of the social unrest. Instead, they hung out with the artists in the lower social class all year around and wrote script for them, which unintentionally contributed to the prosperity of Chinese theater.

Yuan *zaju* was also referred to as northern tune *zaju*, in contrast with southern tune *xiwen*. In Song and Yuan dynasties, there existed a sharp difference in music and theater between South and North. Certainly, southern tune *xiwen* was born earlier than northern tune *zaju*, however, the latter was distinct in its musical system without the impact of the former. Yuan *zaju* did not develop from Song Jin *zaju*, either. Though they had the same name *zaju*, Song Jin *zaju* were small-sized theaters mainly to tease the audience, without complete stories and with music playing a subordinate position. Surely, Song Jin *zaju* and other art form of singing with dancing and small-sized teasing theater were all included in Yuan *zaju*, performing the function of regulating the intense atmosphere and bridge the time gap when the actors change clothes.

Zaju and *xiwen* were both impacted by singing with dancing as zhu gongdiao. A comparison between the surviving fragments of zhu *gongdiao* and Yuan *zaju* with a similar theme shows that Yuan *zaju* followed zhu *gongdiao* in its large size, telling a complete story with various set group tunes and alternating between speaking and singing.

Yuan *zaju* typically had four *zhe* (a unit of theater), preceded with a *xiezi*, an introduction to the theater. There were exceptions, such as *xiezi of Tears on the Blue Gown (Qing Shan Lei)* that is added between the first *zhe* and the second one; in *Orphan of Zhao (Zhao Shi Gu Er)*, xiezi is followed with fifth *zhe*, but the fifth *zhe* is short and can be considered as an end. The so-called four *zhe* were actually four groups of sets with different *gongdiao* from the musical point of view. Every group was composed of several or dozens of *qupai* (a tune) in the same *gongdiao* and was

The mural paint of Guangsheng Temple in Hongtong County, Shanxi Province shows the performance scene of Yuan *zaju*.

The painting of Baoning Temple in Youyu County, Shanxi Province shows that theatrical troupe of the Yuan Dynasty presses on with the journey, bringing musical instruments along with them.

comparatively fixed in form, from which we still could find the overall dramatic pattern. The connection between *qupai*, including its chronological order followed certain rules, controlled by the musical style and the melody of different *qupai*. Furthermore, every group had a common first tune as its introduction. For instance, the first tune of *zheng gongdiao* was usually *duan zhenghao* and *xianlü gong's* was *dian jiangchun*. The first tune was measured in verse, smooth in tune and generally fixed in intonation. The name of the group was a combination of *gongdiao* and the first tune, such as *xianlu · dian jiangchun, shuangdiao · xin shuilling* and *huangzhong · zui huayin*. Also, every group had an end, namely, *shawei* or *shousha*. The function of *shawei* was to end a story. Sometimes, a group of set was ended with several *shawei*, which were arranged in reverse order, such as the third sha, the second sha, the first sha. The group of set of Yuan *zaju* was well-structured and followed a certain program. The first tune, as an introduction and *shawei*, as an end were both integral parts of set group. *Xiezi*, often arranged before four *zhe*, can be considered as a prelude to enter the theater before the main plot, which described the story background or the main characters.

The division of modes mainly lies in *qiang* (the opera's tune) and *ban* (the opera's rhythm) and the change of tunes and rhythms contributes to various styles. Meanwhile, the variety of rhythm with the same mode can be used to express particular feelings, helpful to narrate different events and create distinctive theater occasions. When a set musical group is based on the same mode, the lines should use the same rhyme, forming the general rules that in Yuan *zaju* there are usually four sets of musicals in four *zhe* with the lines employing four different feet. That general rule with four rhymes in four musical sets with variety of lines and tunes to display the ups and downs of the language styles in the entire theater suggests that the dramatists and players were versatile enough to utilize various means to strengthen dramatic effect.

Just like *xiwen*, the Yuan *zaju* have strict role-playing rules. However, the Yuan *zaju* centers on the main male and female characters. Therefore, there are two types with the male actor who plays the main role called Male theater, with the female called Female theater. The singing girls always played the leading role either as women or men. In the records of Yuan brothels, there were not a few singing girls who excelled in playing male characters. Some talented were both good at male and female roles. The singing girls in brothels managed by the government were the main playing groups, which was not a place where singing girls gathered but with only one well-known singing girl who was the mainstay and played with several supportive actors to make her stand out. The entire opera should concentrate only on her performance. Take Ma Zhiyuan's *Autumn in the Han Palace* (*Han Gong Qiu*) and an unknown author's *Zhang Yi's Indifference to Su Qin* (*Dong Su Qin*) for instance. The two theaters both focus on male character and from the very beginning to the end, including the interlude, all are performed by the male role. It is the same with Guan Hanqing's *Official Qian Wisely Treats Lady Xie* (*Qian Da Yin Zhi Chong Xie Tian Xiang*) but with a female as the main role. There is still another opposite sample. In the opera Xue Rengui, the main character Xue is played by a supportive actor, not the main singer. Consequently, there is no performance for him although the story develops around him. As Yuan *zaju* has only one main performer, when arranging the introduction of various roles, the general rule must be taken into account since the main performer should play a role that requires singing and not necessarily play the hero. For example, Shang Zhongxian's *Liu Yi Sending Love Signal in Dongting Lake (Dong Ting Hu Liu Yi Chuan Shu)* is a female-oriented theater. The main female performer plays the heroine in the introduction, the first, third and fourth *zhe* but in the second *zhe* she plays the goddess who is in charge of lightning. In the theater *Xue Rengui*, a male performer plays the part of the official in arms Lord Cai in the first *zhe*, the peer who spent his childhood with Xue in the third, while in the second and fourth the role of Xue's father. The reason for the main performer playing less important parts is that these roles need singing. Furthermore, during the Yuan Dynasty, theaters still followed the general rule with only one main performer in a play.

The performance of *zaju* in Yuan Dynasty carried the conventional traditions and rich ways of performance, integrating music, dance and stunts and creating an admirable performance system. As the *zaju* develops and the audience group enlarges, the theoretical troupe begins to expand and, at the same time, the originally-generalized roles start divide. The role of *dan* (female roles) is gradually subdivided into main, supportive, young, grown, old and funny roles. The *mo* (male roles) are divided into main, young, false and supportive ones.

The specification of roles suggests further specialization of performance, enhancing the artistic level remarkably. We can see the remarkable achievement of Yuan *zaju* through the high degree of specialization.

The large number of Yuan *zaju* is a remarkable achievement, although it is rather difficult to know the exact number. The *Record of Ghost Book (Lu Gui Bu)* written by Zhong Sicheng (around 1279–1360) keeps record of 152 *zaju* playwrights and over 450 works. Jia Zhongming (1343–1422) added 71 more playwrights and 156 more works during the transition between the Yuan and Ming dynasties. Zang Fanxun (1550–1620) during the Ming Dynasty compiled the *Selection of Yuan Theater (Yuan Qu Xuan)*, sorting out 94 kinds *zaju* of

Yuan Dynasty and six kinds of the early Ming Dynasty. Sui Shusen, a contemporary, contributed to the compilation of 62 works of theater in the Yuan and early Ming dynasties, whose transcripts we have a chance to read. They display the prosperity and remarkable achievements of Yuan *zaju*.

Yuan *zaju* has not only great performances but also flows with high literary levels. Speaking of ancient Chinese literary achievements, people always refer to *Tangshi Songci Yuanqu* (poems in Tang Dynasty, *ci* in Song and *zaju* in Yuan), three kinds of literary works. *Yuanqu* is an inclusive name for *sanqu* (a type of verse with tonal patterns modeled on tunes drawn from folk music) and *zaju*. Yuan *zaju* employs both verse and prose, integrating the verse and music into an entire whole to narrate a long story, which shows the playwrights' tremendous ability to master such a complicated writing pattern and create numerous moving and impressive characters.

The content of Yuan *zaju* has been divided into 12 fields, namely, god in fairy world, hermit life, officialdom, martyrs, filial piety, punishing the treacherous, exiled subject and orphan heir, the oppressed class uprise, love romance, gathering and departure, singsong girls and courtesans, Buddha and spirit.

This classification might not be so accurate, but it indicates the basic tendency of playwrights and artists in the Yuan Dynasty.

The most representative among the numerous dramatists are Guan Hanqing, Wang Shifu, Ma Zhiyuan and Bai Pu.

Wang Shifu, a peerless playwright from the Yuan Dynasty with his well-known *Romance of the Western Bower* (*Xi Xiang Ji*) being one of the masterpieces at that time, was born around late 13th century or early 14th century, but little is known about his life. There are only hints from his poems and a rough knowledge usually associated with geishas in the government-managed houses. It is obvious that he, just like his contemporaries, was rather popular among geishas. He created 13 plays, among which *Romance of the Western Bower and A Tumbledown Cave* (*Lü Meng Zheng Feng Xue Po*

Guzici

Guzici is a type of art with talking and speaking popular during the Song Dynasty. It is composed of verse and prose, usually with a small scale. There are ten stanzas in each piece of writing and it gets its name for the performance set to music. Early guzici is sung repeatedly in the same tune, not narrating any story. However, Zhao Lingzhi's Butterfly and Flowers is a kind of guzici singing and telling a story between two young lovers, consisting of one prose speech and a stanza of singing, the singing part uses the same lines repeated 12 times.

Yao Ji) were popular.

Wang's *Romance of the Western Bower* is based on *Zhu Gongdiao of Romance of the Western Bower*, and collected its materials from Yuan Zhen's (a poet from the Tang Dynasty) *Story of Yingying* (*Ying Ying Zhuan*). Meanwhile, during the Song Dynasty Zhao Lingzhi (1061–1134) produced *guzici Butterfly and Flowers*. Dong Jieyuan during the Jin Dynasty brought it into a complete and touching story through his various modes. What's more, Wang's *zaju Romance of the Western Bower* made it a household representative play.

Romance of the Western Bower describes how the daughter of Premier Cui during the Tang Dynasty and her mother take Premier Cui's coffin back home for burial and face battles along the way. They have to make a short stay in the famous Pujiu Temple. Zhang Junrui, who was going for the imperial examination, happens to pass by and encounters young Lady Cui by chance in the Buddha hall. Appreciating her beauty, he decides to drop by the temple, seizing the chance to meet the beauty. At the same time, however, the gangster group leader Sun Feihu heard of Lady Cui's breathtaking beauty and besieges the temple, intending to take Lady Cui violently. Out of anxiety, the Mother of Yingying (the young lady's name) announces the betrothal of her daughter to whoever can rescue them. Zhang stands out bravely, writing to his old friend and persuading him to send forces to frighten the gangsters away. Old Lady Cui takes the engagement as a matter of expediency for the urgent situation and now, having been rescued, she plans to break her own word. Frustrated, Zhang feels hopeless and falls ill. Yingying, however, holds good feelings towards

The illustration of *Romance of the West Bower*. In the picture, the heroine, Cui Yingying is reading a letter from her beloved, while her handmaiden Hongniang is peeping behind a screen.

Zhang and feels guilty about her mother's breach. The two begin a secret affair. A month later, with Lady Cui sees something between them and asks Yingying's servant what is going on between them. The handmaiden Hongniang has to tell the truth and tries to lead Lady Cui into accepting the reality, allowing their marriage. Lady Cui has no choice but to accept their union. Nevertheless, Lady Cui declares that the Cui family is of a high status and Zhang must go for the imperial examination and win an official position, gaining the permission to marry Yingying with pompous rituals. Zhang and Yingying are separated. After the departure, Yingying's spirit accompanies Zhang all the way to success. Finally, Zhang succeeds in the exam and wins happiness for them. The story finishes in a happy ending.

This play describes the natural love between two young people, the pure love and gorgeous words won remarkable praise from the

The stage photo of Kunqu Opera *Romance of the West Bower*. It is staged in the Northern Kunqu Opera Theatre.

onset. Wang is adept at exhibiting unexpressive emotions through most representative details. For example, when narrating that Zhang and Yingying could not get closer even when nearby, the smart handmaiden Hongniang sang the following:

> *Languish as the handsome male with wrinkles on forehead,*
> *The beauty not the same as before, with the waist slimmer and*
> *the clothes looser,*
> *One drowsy without any attention on the book,*
> *One absent-minded without intention to do embroidery;*
> *One playing the complaining tunes on the instrument showing*
> *inner lovesickness,*
> *One writing heartbroken lines on the paper with soft*
> *expectations;*
> *The same lovesickness for both.*

When seeing off Zhang, Yingying's singing part is rich in the color of nature to offset her sadness and reluctance to part. It quickly became a classic literary stanza:

> *With clouds the sky turns grey, over yellow-blow-paved way.*
> *How bitter blows the western breeze! From north to south fly the*
> *wild geese. Why like wine-flushed face is frosted forest red? It's*
> *dyed in tears parting lovers shed.*
> *So late we meet, so soon we part; the long willow branch cannot*
> *tie the rein, wishing the sun fixed on the branch with time without*
> *flying; the horse runs fast in the front, while the carriage follows*
> *after; without our feeling talking open we pretended to avoid*
> *suspicion, with our love public, parting coming so soon. Hearing*
> *you departing, I have no intention to make up; seeing the departing*
> *place, I lose weight for missing you so much. Who knows my inner*
> *complaint?*

When describing the love between the two young lovers, the

process and change of emotions are both rather complicated. At the very beginning, it is Zhang who chases Yingying on his mind; while on the departure scene, Yingying demonstrates her tender feelings singing the following:

> *With mountain views around, the whip echoes in the sunset. Lovesickness more than all annoyance in the world preoccupies my mind, and how could the small carriage carry it? I will write to you as frequent as possible, and you need not swear not to come back without reputation. There is still one thing you should bear in mind that you never stay anywhere like here far away.*

The difference between the desire of Yingying and Zhang indicates the setbacks on the road to their marriage. Through the entire plot, their love crisis usually takes place with a previous omen. The barrier to marriage not only lies in their family, but more dramatic is Yingying's thirst for love and hesitation to accept love when facing Zhang's pursuit, which adds much more thought-provoking ups and downs. This makes the story rich in feeling.

Great writers can always expose human nature that is hardly seen through details. We can see the gender differences, its importance and human nature more than the gap in beliefs between two generations through a happy ending and sweet love.

Wang's *Romance of Western Bower* differs from other , not finishing a story in four acts but with twenty acts in five chapters. There are some suspicions of whether the fifth act was actually written by Wang since the essence is mainly distributed in the first four chapters. Still, Wang's *Romance of Western Bower* has been performed on stage in various forms at different times since the Yuan Dynasty.

Ma Zhiyuan is another significant playwright from the Yuan Dynasty and his well-received *Autumn in the Han Palace* (*Han Gong Qiu*) is placed the first in the Selection of Yuan Theater. It is worth special attention.

The play concentrates mainly on the tragic love between Emperor Yuandi in Han Dynasty and Wang Zhaojun (the most beautiful lady at that time). Wang was born in an ordinary family but is lucky enough to be selected into the palace to become one of the numerous wife-to-be for the emperor. However, she would not bribe the imperial painter Mao Yanshou who is responsible for painting images of those ladies. As a result, Mao makes her look ugly so she doesn't get the chance to wait on the emperor. However, Zhaojun could play the *pipa* (a four-stringed Chinese lute) quite well. One day the emperor was attracted by the sound of *pipa* and called her in. By accident, He finds out about Zhaojun's great beauty and she becomes his favorite. As a result, what Mao had done was exposed and he has to flee into the Fan tribe, where he instigates the tribe leader to ask for Wang Zhaojun as his wife, otherwise, he would start a war. As the officials cannot think of strategies to defend the empire against the tribe, the emperor has to give up Zhaojun despite enjoying her company. Without Zhaojun, the emperor feels lonely and becomes preoccupied by the missing beauty.

The illustration of *Autumn in the Han Palace*. It shows Wang Zhaojun departs the frontier as a peace-weaver.

Autumn in the Han Palace was mainly performed by a male character who plays the part of the emperor and sings from the start to the end. Despite that, this play remains a classic. After sending Zhaojun to the Fan tribe, the emperor is miserable and annoyed. That was vividly described by Ma Zhiyuan:

Facing the wild with the withered grass on frost, people carrying spears, horses loading essentials, carriage taking army provisions, paddock being enclosed, she bid farewell to her lord, and I had to say goodbye. Since then she belonged to the wild outside and I went back to the palace. Back to the palace, through the layers of gates, along the corridors, near the bedroom, at dusk, lonely and cold evening, with the green window screen, I cannot stop missing her, my lady! Oh, without missing unless I was iron-hearted, still with tears rolling down continuously. The picture of my lady will stay with me tonight.

This episode describes the miserable feelings of the emperor and makes audiences shed sympathetic tears.

This play is not a usual romance tragedy, as made clear by the focus on special plots. Its summit does not lie in the loving days the hero and heroine spent together, but in the strong suffering and longing for Zhaojun after their separation. As an emperor in a kingdom, Yuandi was not able to keep his concubine by his side. His feelings are not only based on their separation but more in the weakness of his kingdom, resulting in the humiliation of sending his concubine to keep peace rather than face losing a war.

Orphan of Zhao (Zhao Shi Gu Er) by Ji Junxiang is an influential theater from the

A stage photo of Peking Opera *Orphan of Zhao.*

Shaoxing Opera *Orphan of Zhao* performed by Shanghai Yue Opera Troupe.

Yuan Dynasty that takes the story in Spring and Autumn Period, telling of many warriors that make great sacrifices to protect the orphan heir of a city state, especially focusing on an old man's endurance of humiliation and responsibility to raise the child and take revenge at last.

Orphan of Zhao is transcribed from this and has been well-received since. In 1731 the French churchman Joseph Ma translated the play into French and in 1775 Voltaire re-translated it into *Chinese Orphan*. This play and a theater *The Chalk Circle* (*Hui Lan Ji*) are excellent theaters introduced into the Western world.

Guan Hanqing's Remarkable Achievement

There are many famous writers from the Yuan Dynasty and Guan Hanqing was no doubt the most talented. We do not know exactly the years of his life, but he lived around the 13th century during the transition from the Jin to the Yuan Dynasty. It is said that once he worked as a court physician or might have been an

A portrait of Guan Hanqing.

ordinary doctor in the capital city.

Experiencing many difficulties through his life but with a straightforward temperament, he declared that "I am the leader of both honorable men and prodigals" and even claimed that "I am a genuine bronze bean that cannot be boiled into pieces or stewed thoroughly or beaten flat or fried cracking."

During his life, he was given the title of "the leader of *liyuan* (a place for artistic performance), the composers and the dramatists," which suggests his significance in Yuan opera.

Guan Hanqing created more than 60 theaters and there are complete scripts for 18. *The Injustice to Dou E* (*Dou E Yuan*) is one of his most influential masterpieces. *Preparing a Fish for Mid-Autumn Festival* (*Wang Jiang Ting Zhong Qiu Qie Kuai*), *Zhao Pan'er Rescued Her Sisters via Smart Tricks* (*Zhao Pan Er Feng Yue Jiu Feng Chen*), *The Pavilion of Praying to the Moon* (*Gui Yuan Jia Ren Bai Yue Ting*), *Bao Daizhi Has Lu Beheaded Wisely* (*Bao Dai Zhi Zhi Zhan Lu Zhai Lang*), and *Sire Guan Kept Appointment at Dinner of Treachery* (*Guan Da Wang Du Fu Dan Dao Hui*) are all fantastic examples.

In *The Injustice to Dou E*, the heroine is a young widow who marries into the Cai family when her father goes for the imperial examination. Her husband dies young and she then lives with her old and weak mother-in-law, who makes living lending money. One day Doctor Sai intends to repudiate his debt by killing the old woman when old lady Cai goes to get her payment. A father and son named Zhang pass by and save her life. Lady Cai invites them to her house to thank them.

Shaanxi Opera *The Injustice to Dou E*. In the picture, the unjustly accused Dou E is dispatched to the execution ground.

However, the father and son have evil ideas in mind, trying to force Dou E and her mother-in-law into marrying them. Dou E refuses their offer. The young Zhang then thinks of poisoning Lady Cai. However, Lady Cai does not drink the poisoned soup instead but Old Zhang does and dies. The Young Zhang brings a false charge against Lady Cai for poisoning his father after failing to marry Dou E.

Without any questioning or solid evidence, the official employs cruel torture on Lady Cai. Dou E has to take the false charge herself in order to prevent her mother-in-law from being tortured. As a result, Dou E is sentenced to death. On the execution ground, she makes three oaths: That her blood will spot the white tape, that it will snow in June and that there will be drought for three years. She says God will hear her grievance and will make these things happen to bear witness. As expected, after her death, her three oaths become reality one by one. Meanwhile, her father

Puzhou Clapper Opera *The Injustice to Dou E*. Here shows that Dou E's lost soul meets with her long-separated father.

Dou Tianzhang finds great success during the exam and wins the trust of the court. He is assigned to visit different places. When he arrives in Chuzhou, which had been suffering from a three-year drought, he dreams of his daughter's spirit—whom he hadn't seen for 16 years—pouring out her grievance. Later Dou Tianzhang investigates the case, punishes the real murderer and the fatuous official. Although Dou E is finally given justice, she cannot return to life.

This theater mainly centers on a fragile woman's grievance, which is displayed in Guan's many works. His sympathy towards helpless women in the lower classes is a common theme. Dou E is the most representative among them. She was insulted in the court, in the descriptive words "just awake and then faint, suffering various beatings, one more staff, one more blood trail and more skin off." When tied to the execution place, Guan designed the lines for Dou E to express loudly her grievance:

There is no reason to breach the law and the false charge has to
be taken. A cry for righting the grievance can touch just nature.
In a rather short time, I am sentenced to death, how could I bear
the injustice without any complaints? There is the sun and the
moon for the day and night, and there is master who is in control
of life and death. Master in the world should be capable of telling
right and wrong, but the exact right and wrong were completely
opposite-vice being rewarded and virtue being punished. Oh, God
of Heaven and Earth, you should be so to bully the weak and fear
the strong. God of Earth, you cannot tell right from wrong, and
God of Heaven, you reward the vice and punish the virtue. How
could that be your duty like that? Oh, only leaving me with tears
rolling…

In the fourth act, the spirit of Dou E goes on the stage, singing "every day I wait with tears at the place to look at my hometown, eagerly waiting for the murderer, walking slowly in darkness, floating in the hurricane, and being locked and lost in the frog and cloud."

The description of Dou E's feelings of grievance is extremely appropriate. However, Guan not only takes notice of the fragile women's lives but also emphasizes the heroine's kindheartedness. In the theater, we can see that Dou E takes the false charge out of filial piety for her mother-in-law, not like many who couldn't endure the cruel torture themselves to confess falsely, but confessed all when she saw her mother-in-law might be tortured.

When facing execution, her only request was to take a back way fearing her mother-in-law's suffering when seeing her on her way to execution. When her father gives her justice, her only wish was that her father could take care of her mother-in-law. Being in a quandary, she kept in mind not her own life and safety but how to lessen the detriment to both body and mind of her old mother-in-law through her own sacrifice.

Therefore, the play quoted the story of *Filial Daughter-in-law in East China Sea* (*Dong Hai Xiao Fu*), to indicate the heroine

Hebei Clapper Opera *The Injustice to Dou E*. In the picture, the gracefully floating opera-water sleeve vividly shows the grievance of Dou E, successfully achieving a fantastic stage effect.

and her tremendous actions to move and touch the Heaven and Earth are rooted in her filial piety. Furthermore, her elder was not a blood relative and that strengthens her piety and kindheartedness.

The Injustice to Dou E shows the author's great mastery in expressions as well. For example, Doctor Sai says "having a second thought when treating the sick, to offer medicine according to an old famous medicine book; the died is cast while the alive is done." The fatuous official always bent his knee to people who bent on the ground, explained like that when the servant couldn't understand, "you should know that the people who came to bring a lawsuit are the bread and meal to me." When questioning the case, he only knows how to use torture, saying "men are worthless creatures, never confess without any beating. Servant, choose a large staff to keep on beating."

The characters are played by *Jing* roles, with exaggerated words in a strongly ironic atmosphere, causing people to laugh. The most outstanding feature of Guan's work is that he could follow the strict rules of rhythm even though he used common language in his plays.

From the above introduction, with Guan as representative during the Yuan Dynasty, playwrights tended to select materials close to the tastes of the lower classes and familiar to the public, thus creating plays that could reach thousands of people. Meanwhile, as they were skilful in employing idioms and folk sayings in their singing lines and soliloquy, they ensured idioms and accents from the Song and Yuan times flourished and produced shining attributes.

Refinement and Elegance: *Chuanqi* of the Ming and Qing Dynasties and the Times of Kunqu Opera

Scholars' Renovate of *Xiwen*

Zaju from the Yuan Dynasty proved the greatness of Chinese operas. The creative and performance centre of *zaju* during the Yuan Dynasty gradually shifted from the north to the south. It did not take long for Wenzhou, where scripts of *xiwen* were born, and its neighbour Lin'an, the ancient capital of the Southern Song Dynasty, to become China's most important opera centers. However, *zaju* used northern tunes as its major means of music expression and did not appeal to the aesthetic tastes of southerners.

In China's vast south, *xiwen* were once typically low key but some works spread. During the late Yuan and early Ming dynasties, *xiwen* re-emerged. But, in order to replace the northern *zaju* and the literary masters, xiwen could not rely on their originally vulgar styles. One successful example was *Story of the Pipa (Pi Pa Ji)* written by Gao Ming. Gao elevated southern *xiwen* from the realm of folklore with eminent literary achievements and gradually replaced *zaju* in the north, contributing new symbolic masterpieces to the development of Chinese operas and ushered a new ear in Chinese opera.

Gao Ming was born early year in the 14th century and died during the late Yuan or early Ming Dynasty. At the age of 40, Gao served as a minor official but retired quickly. Moving to Lishe town, in the east of Ningbo, Gao wrote his great work *Story of the Pipa*. It has been said that in order to write the play, he worked and slept in a small building for the three years it took him to finish the work and the floor under the path of his feet was worn down.

Story of the Pipa told the joys and sorrows of Zhao Wuniang and Cai Bojie. As early as the Song Dynasty, it was produced as an opera. In the xiwen work *Chaste Woman Zhao and Cai Erlang*, Cai Bojie leaves home for the capital in search of an official position. However, after his efforts meet with success, he abandons his family. Lighting finally kills him. The story delves deeply into civilian ethics and values.

The southern *xiwen* of the Song and Yuan dynasties were the
art forms of the lowest ranks of society. They showed a clear
distinction between love and hate but lacked the voice of the
literati. Gao Ming, as was common among scholars, rewrote the
story. He kept the original content and sympathetic character of
Zhao Wuniang but placed the focus on Cai Bojie. The in-depth
exploration of the psychology of Cai Bojie enriched the story. The
previous works of the story all focused on the tragic life of Zhao
Wuniang. However, in Gao Ming's *Story of the Pipa*, another center
emerges: The three disobediences of Cai Bojie.

A significant change in *Story of the Pipa* lies in the emergence of
Cai Bojie as a dutiful son. Although officials wanted to recruit him,
he refused for the sake of his parents. His father reprimanded him,
telling him to value his prospects and not rely on family love and
affection, and feel reluctant to leave home, Cai Bojie bid farewell
to his parents and his wife and left for the capital to take part
in the imperial examination. He won the first place. Difficulties
quickly ensued. The emperor wanted to preside over the wedding
ceremony of the daughter of a Grand Mentor named Niu and
ordered Cai Bojie to marry her. Cai Bojie used many excuses to
refuse the marriage to no avail. Finally, he asked to see the emperor
and said he could not serve as the official but just hoped to return
home to serve his parents. However, the Grand Mentor used his
influence over the court to overlook the fact that Cai Bojie had
a wife and elderly parents. He urged the emperor to refuse his
request, causing Cai Bojie's wife and parents to suffer at the hands
of fate.

Refusing the examination, marriage and an official rank—the
three disobediences—changed the hardhearted Cai Bojie into a
helpless Cai Bojie, who won the first in the imperial examination,
but was eager to go home, who stayed at Niu's residence, but
missed his parents and virtuous wife, and became depressed. He
sang: "The old chord has been broken, but I am not accustomed to
the new one. It is impossible to have the old chord again, but I will

Kunqu Opera *Story of the Pipa*, Cai Bojie and Miss Niu get married, performed by Jiangsu Suzhou Kunqu Troupe.

fight hard after getting rid of the new chord. I tried, but again was confused by officials."

The dramatic process of *Story of the Pipa* constantly highlights Cai Bojie's anxiety, showing his virtuous character. Using this indirect way to justify his behaviour to abandon his parents and wife, of course, requires superb literary imagination.

The original leading character in this story is Zhao Wuniang, but Gao Ming made Cai Bojie an important part of the sad story and changed the simple concept idea of a separated husband and wife into an antagonistic couple. As a result, the story changes considerably. In the story, Zhao's distraught kindness is not affected by Cai Bojie's changing image. In the new version, Zhao is more touching than any previous incarnation.

Starting from Cai Bojie's departure from home, *Story of the Pipa* advances with two parallel storylines in two different locales.

The story uses appreciation of the lotus, moon and other scenarios to express the deep concern and longing of Cai Bojie. It also adopts eating chaff, shaving off hair to be a nun, and other behaviour to describe Zhao's hardships. In her hometown, Zhao ate chaff and preserved vegetables and left the remaining grain to her parents-in-law. The different parts of the eating chaff scene show double significance:

> *Vomiting makes me painful with tears, and my throat was even stuffed. Oh, chaff! You were milled and screened just like my pains, experiencing great hardships. Bitter person eats bitterness, witnessing the two kinds of bitterness meeting, but you may not know it is hard to swallow.*
>
> *Chaff and rice are essentially mutually dependent, but they are separated by winnows. One is mean and the other is noble, just like me and my husband having no chance to meet again. My husband, you are rice. You are somewhere else, but nowhere for me to look for you. I am exactly the chaff, how could I save others from hunger with chaff? Just as you have left, how could I serve my parents-in-law with good foods?*

Zhao's parents-in-law felt sad and passed away one after the other in quick succession. Without any way to earn a living, she had to cut her hair to sell and earn money to bury her parents-in-laws. Gao Ming arranged for her to eat chaff, making people naturally think of chaff and husks—the well known metaphor for poor wife.

The hair-cutting symbology included plenty of realistic elements and left plenty of space for the audiences to have afterthoughts. Because in Chinese traditional culture, hair is a symbol that usually refers to the first formal marriage between a man and a woman. Zhao sold her hair to seek help and even used her clothes to wrap soil and erect tomb to bury her parents-in-law. She went to the capital with a *pipa* in her arms and got help from Ms Niu, the same kind lady and the couple finally reunited. Ms Niu persuaded her father, and her father agreed to allow Cai Bojie to resign from his

Kunqu Opera *Story of the Pipa*, Zhao Wuniang eats chaff and leaves remaining grain to her parents-in-law, making them moved and feel guilty, performed by Jiangsu Suzhou Kunqu Troupe.

official post and return to his hometown to offer a sacrifice to his parents.

The long story makes up for the regretful—and practically impossible—ending in which Cai Bojie takes his two wives to sweep his parents' tombs.

The greatness of *Story of the Pipa* lies in that the author did not avoid the three unfilial aspects of Cai Bojie's story—failure to serve his parents when alive, bury his parents when dead, and offer a sacrifice to his parents after burial—but he tried to make the audience feel sympathy rather than merely hate Cai Bojie. Therefore, he succeeded in establishing the common aesthetic foundation between scholars and common people.

The emergence of *Story of the Pipa* changed the basic structure and ethical values of the common ungrateful scholar plays common among xiwen during the Song and Yuan dynasties. Equally important, *Story of the Pipa* includes 42 scenes, completely

changing the pattern of four scenes of *zaju* during the Yuan
Dynasty constrained by a musical system.

The author could use more dramatic ways to start the plot. As
the touching story covers the narration of two roles at the same
time, so it initiated the start of the dual structure of the *chuanqi*
during the Ming and Qing dynasties. It completely changed the
cultural status of the scripts of xiwen. Zhu Yuanzhang, the first
emperor (reigned 1368–1398) of the Ming Dynasty thought highly
of it, saying "the *Four Books and Five Classics* is daily necessities
such as food and clothing which every family has; *Story of the Pipa*
is like a delicacy, wealth and noble families can not do without it."

The scripts of *xiwen* starting from the Song Dynasty rose in
stature thanks to *Story of the Pipa*, and soon replaced the *zaju* from
the Yuan Dynasty to become the most influential opera form in
China during the Ming and Qing dynasties. Starting with *Story of
the Pipa*, Chinese operas entered the cultural mainstream from the
bottom and the outside edges of society to integrate them into the

Kunqu Opera *A Wooden Hairpin*, Aunt Qian takes betrothal gifts from Sun and Wang's families
to Yulian's bedroom, and speaks highly of Sun's wealth, but Yulian insists on choosing the
wooden hairpin of Wang's, performed by Jiangsu Kunqu Troupe.

conscious development process of Chinese culture.

A Wooden Hairpin (*Jing Chai Ji*), *White Rabbit* (*Bai Tu Ji*), *Praying to the Moon* (*Bai Yue Ji*), and *Killing the Dog* (*Sha Gou Ji*) are the most important opera creations from the early Ming Dynasty after *Story of the Pipa*. The emergence of these four major plays further consolidated the position of *xiwen*.

A Wooden Hairpin tells the story of a young woman named Qian Yulian who refuses to marry to a very rich man named Sun Ruquan and marries Wang Shipeng, a scholar who takes *a wooden hairpin* as a betrothal gift. After getting married, Wang goes to the capital to attend the imperial examination and is successful. Wang is then pushed into marrying Moqi's daughter but, after refusing, he is banished. The conflicts grow from there as Sun Ruquan alters a letter from Wang to Qian Yulian into a divorce announcement. As a result, Qian Yulian's stepmother steps in and forces Qian to remarry. Qian refuses and jumps into the river, but is saved by Qian Zaihe, a newly appointed official. In turn, Qian Zaihe adopts Qian Yulian as his foster daughter, taking her to his official residence. His actions are based on mistaken information that Wang Shipeng is dead. Both members of the couple believe the other to be dead but still long for each other. Fate steps in, however, and the two fortuitously meet by the river while offering a sacrifice to each other. Fortunately, they met with each other when offering sacrifice to each other by the river.

White Rabbit is also known as *Liu Zhiyuan*. As early as the Tang Dynasty, there was *Zhu Gongdiao of Liu Zhiyuan*. It told the story that *Liu Zhiyuan* left home to join the army while his wife, Sanniang, was tortured at home by his brother and sister-in-law. Sanniang gave birth to a son in the mill. She used her mouth to bite the umbilical cord off and named him Yaojilang, meaning his umbilical chord was bitten off. She asked Dou Gong to send her son to *Liu Zhiyuan*. Fifteen years later, *Liu Zhiyuan* asked his son to return to visit his mother. His son did not know where to find his mother, until he meets her drawing water from a well when he

Shaoxing Opera *White Rabbit*, Sanniang and her son meet again after 15 years of separation, performed by Zhejiang Wenzhou Shaoxing Opera Troupe.

hunts a *white rabbit*. In turn, *Liu Zhiyuan* returns to the village with his men and reunites with his wife.

Praying to the Moon is also known as *Story of the Quiet Bower* (*You Ge Ji*). Guan Hanqing wrote the original *The Pavilion of Praying to the Moon*. The story was written amidst the ravages and turmoil of war. In the story, Jiang Shilong and Wang Ruilan meet while fleeing for their safety and get married. They experience joys and sorrows. The best parts of this work are incorporated into the southern *xiwen Praying to the Moon*. The librettos of the roles are simple and vivid, maintaining the essence of the original work.

Killing the Dog also developed based on *Killing the Dog to Persuade Husband* (*Sha Gou Quan Fu*), a *zaju* from the Yuan Dynasty that follows the same plot lines. Sun Hua, the son of a wealthy family, plots with two local riffraff named Liu Longqing and Hu Zichuan to drive his brother Sun Rong off his family. Sun Hua's wife Yang Yuezhen tries to persuade Sun Hua but fails. So she

A stage photo of Kunqu Opera *Killing the Dog*, performed by Zhejiang Yongjia Conservatory of Kunqu Opera.

kills a dog, puts it in a bag, and places it outside the gate. Sun Hua returns home late at night and is frightened. To avoid lawsuits, he asks Liu Longqing and Hu Zichuan to help him. But those two are fair-weather friends and avoid Sun Hua. The only one willing to help is Sun Rong, showing the family the affection of brothers. The story was often told during the Song and Yuan dynasties. Besides the detailed descriptions of family affection, the description of Liu Longqing and Hu Zichuan and other local riffraff was especially vivid.

These four southern xiwen each have unique characteristics. Along with *Story of the Pipa* they marked the splendid beginning of the era of the *chuanqi*, the new stage of development in Chinese operas.

Kunqu Opera and Exquisite *Peony Pavilion*

The use of the word *chuanqi* derived from the Tang Dynasty, but the concept of *chuanqi* during the Tang and Song referred to short odd stories. From the emergence of *xiwen* during the Song and Yuan dynasties, the word *chuanqi* was used for as a general term for the opera style of narration of offbeat stories.

From *The No.1 Scholar Zhang Xie* during the Song Dynasty to *Story of the Pipa* in early Yuan Dynasty, the system of scripts shared similarities and differences with *zaju*. They narrated a complete story in the form of tunes alternated with monologue and they adopted *qupai* style music as the core means for lyrical characters.

However, *zaju* consists of four scenes and the *qupai* used by each part is strictly constrained by the palace tunes, while the *qupai* selection for *chuanqi* shows more flexibility. From *The No.1 Scholar Zhang Xie*, which is not divided into different scenes, to *Story of the Pipa* consisting of 42 scenes, the script of *xiwen* is longer than that of *zaju* and incorporates more content.

Using the changes in palace tunes to divide the play into four scenes seems improper. Breaking the restrictions on palace tunes and the number of scenes, especially the one-role lead restriction, and focusing more on the dramatic features instead of the musical perspective are the new characteristics of *xiwen*, commonly known as *chuanqi* during the Ming Dynasty.

Chuanqi include more foreshadowing than *zaju* dramatic features and have musical styles that are harder to regulate. The authors of *chuanqi* were mainly scholars, so they pursued the same perfect music expression as operas, setting the direction for dramatists during the Ming Dynasty. At that time, Wei Liangfu of Taicang, Jangsu, focused his efforts on xiwen for a decade and created exquisite Kunshan tune, providing a new means of music for operas. When Wei Liangfu created Kunshan tune, the term *chuanqi* referred to plays created for the performance of the music form using Kunshan tune.

The emergence and development of *xiwen* during the Song and Yuan dynasties focused on Zhejiang. The musical styles are closer to the southern styles. If we believe that different geographical environments lead to different folk customs and even different forms of music, dance and operas, then as southern *xiwen* replaced northern *zaju* to become a major component of Chinese opera it inevitably lead to changes in mainstream music styles.

Indeed, during the era of *chuanqi* of the Ming Dynasty, in the massive regions of the south, a variety of tunes sprang up, such as the Haiyan tune near Hangzhou in Zhejiang and the Yiyang tune in Jiangxi, which replaced northern *zaju*.

When Wei Liangfu renovated the Kunshan tune, he changed the original arias of Yiyang and Haiyan tunes and used Kunshan tune melodies to establish palace tune and rhythms of the southern and northern styles, incorporating the styles from the south of the Yangtze River that prevailed at the time.

The difference between the southern *xiwen* and northern *zaju* lies in the melody and the accompaniment instruments. Relative to the northern *zaju*, which focuses on plucked string instruments for accompaniment, southern *xiwen* takes the flute as its major musical instrument. The flute's sound is clear and soft.

The work *Washing Silken Gauze* (*Huan Sha Ji*), written by Liang Chenyu, shows the possibility of using Kunshan tune throughout an entire opera and marks the birth of Kunqu Opera, along with new achievements in the musical expression of Chinese operas.

Liang Chenyu, an important dramatist in the 16th century, was born in Kunshan, Jiangsu. *Washing Silken Gauze* was based on *Spring and Autumn of the States of Wu and Yue* (*Wu Yue Chun Qiu*). It includes 45 scenes that explore the competition between Wu and Yue during the Spring and Autumn Period. The State of Wu defeated the State of Yue and King Goujian of Yue adopted a stratagem devised by Fan Li, a senior official, to concede defeat and offer great gifts to the King of Wu, even at the cost of sending Fan Li's fiancee Xi Shi, a stunning beauty.

The King of Wu loved pleasure and neglected state affairs while King Goujian slept on brushwood and tasted gall every day and tried his best. In the end, the State of Yue became strong and

A stage photo of Kunqu Opera *Washing Silken Gauze*, performed by Northern Kunqu Troupe.

overcame its humiliation.

The author abandoned the orientation traditionally used in *zaju* of the Yuan Dynasty that sought simple scripts and pursued elegant scripts with complex rhetoric. It integrated exquisite *shuimo* tune (water mill tune) from Kunqu Opera and attracted a generation of scholars.

After that, *chuanqi-style* literary creations followed norms adopted for Kunshan tune. *Chuanqi* performed with Kunshan tune catered to scholarly tastes in their literal expressions and musical features. They won great favor and became elegant music with special cultural status. Other local tunes of the same period, by comparison, were considered vulgar. Thus, the authentic representative of Chinese elegance shifted from palace music to the Kunqu Opera enjoyed by scholar-bureaucrats.

From the beginning of the mid-Ming Dynasty, the significance and development of Kunqu Opera spread widely and gradually

Kunqu Opera *Return to Life* from *Peony Pavilion*, Liu Mengmei opened the coffin in the tomb, and Du Lininag revived after death. The two get married in the end.

became a symbol of Chinese culture.

The emergence of Tang Xianzu (1550–1616) helped *chuanqi* reach its artistic peak. Tang Xianzu, a famous Ming Dynasty scholar, was well-known for his *Four Dreams at Linchuan*, which included four outstanding plays that displayed his literary achievements. The four plays were *Tale of the Wooden Hairpin* (*Jing Chai Ji*), *Peony Pavilion* (*Mu Dan Ting*), *Nanke Dream* (*Nan Ke Ji*) and *Handan Dream* (*Han Dan Ji*). They shared a common theme of dreams. *Peony Pavilion*, also known as *Revival of Du Liniang* (*Huan Hun Ji*), may be the most outstanding *chuanqi* of the Ming Dynasty.

Peony Pavilion consists of 55 scenes that focus on the erotic desires of Du Liniang, the daughter of Du Bao, governor of Nan'an. Du Liniang dreams of a young scholar she meets in a *Peony Pavilion*. Deeply moved by this dream, she takes a stroll in the garden and suddenly falls ill. She paints portraits, writes a poem and tells her maid to hide these below a stone in the Taihu Lake by the plum tree.

In the Kunqu film *Interrupted Dream*, shot in 1960, famous female role in Peking Opera Mei Lanfang (right) plays the role of Du Liniang, whose student Yan Huizhu plays the role of Chunxiang. The 67-year-old Mei Lanfang is still enchanting with his gracefulness.

A stage photo of Kunqu Opera *Peony Pavilion*, performed by Suzhou Kunqu Troupe.

Shortly after, Du Liniang dies and is buried by the plum tree in the garden. Three years later, a scholar named Liu Mengmei comes into town to participate in the imperial examination. When he falls ill and looks for a cure in a small shrine, he finds the painting of a beautiful girl—the picture of Du Liniang. That night, he dreams of her. Liniang asks him to revive her. Opening her coffin, Liu Mengmei revives Du Liniang. The two lovers decide to get married and go to the capital of that time—Lin'an (present-day Hangzhou).

After passing the examination, Liu Mengmei visits Liniang's father and tells him about the revival but the father accuses Liu Mengmei of being a grave robber, apprehends him and sends him to Lin'an. Unexpectedly, Liu Mengmei wins first place in the imperial examination but Du Bao refused to accept her daughter's marriage considering her to be a devil. However, the emperor himself believes Du Linaing and allows the marriage.

Of all the marvels of *Peony Pavilion*, the most representative is Du Liniang's life and death. A young girl dreams up a great love.

The dream lover is false, but unexpectedly, the man in her dream is a scholar who revives her years later. Du Liniang dies for her dream lover but is revived by a loyal one.

This odd love reaches the limits between life and death. Tang Xianzu's diction shows sparkling ideas. One great example can be found in the lyrics used to describe Du Liniang's erotic desires and hidden bitterness:

> *Already, bright purple and passion pink bloom in profusion, yet to crumbling well, faded walls, such splendour is abandoned. But in this glorious season, where are the sounds of joy in this garden? Mornings take wing, evenings unfold; beyond green arbor, rosy clouds soar. In windy strands of rain, gilded pleasure boats nod in misty waves. Maidens shielded by broached screens, are blinded to such glorious scenes!*
>
> *All over the verdant hill, the azaleas are in full bloom. Beyond trellis vines, silky mist softly lingers. The peony is gorgeous, but blooms late when spring is gone.*

Peony Pavilion marks the peak of artistic achievement in *chuanqi* of the Ming and Qing dynasties. Despite displaying less precision in terms of Tang Xianzu's mastery of the rhythms of Kunqu Opera, and even criticism and taunts from dramatists with more familiar command of the rhythms of Kunqu Opera, *Peony Pavilion* reveals extraordinary talent and quickly became one of the most popular representative plays of Kunqu Opera.

Generations of performing artists' efforts have helped the play reach unparalleled artistic realms in rhetoric, tune, music, movement and performance. It has a lot of staged highlights. Remaining examples of Kunqu Opera performances are widespread and include *The Schoolroom (Gui Shu)*, *Interrupted Dream (Jing Meng)*, *Pursuing the Dream (Xun Meng)*, *The Portrait (Xie Zhen)*, *Soul Departs (Li Hun)*, *Infernal Judgment (Ming Pan)*, *Finding the Portrait (Shi Hua)*, *Union in the Shades (You Gou)*, *The Pledge (Ming*

Shi), and *Return to Life* (*Huan Hun*), are widespread.

Palace of Eternity and *Peach Blossom Fan*

From the beginning of the mid-Ming Dynasty, Kunqu Opera grew in popularity as a result of a number of excellent works.

One was *Palace of Eternity* (*Chang Sheng Dian*), written by Hong Sheng (1645-1704), who was born in Qiantang, Zhejiang. His literary talent was exceptional, but he suffered from great hardship and drifted to the capital to make a living selling scripts. The *Palace of Eternity* was a masterpiece Hong Sheng wrote after more than ten years of effort. It was based on three drafts. It was first called Chenxiang Pavilion, then renamed Dancing with Pretty Garments, and finally *Palace of Eternity*. The play included 50 different scenes and an entire performance lasted two days.

Palace of Eternity focuses on the love between Li Longji, emperor Minghuang of the Tang Dynasty and his concubine Yang Yuhuan, as well as the various connections in those troubled times. It does not conceal the distress brought by Li Longji to the nation for his

A stage photo of Kunqu Opera *Palace of Eternity*, performed by Suzhou Kunqu Troupe.

Palace of Eternity, performed by Zhejiang Hangzhou Kunqu Troupe on Dec.24, 2004 in memory
of the 360 anniversary of the birth of Hong Sheng

excess love for Yang Yuhuan. In the first half of the play, the author
focuses on the description of the love between them, including Li
Longji, his excess love of Yang Yuhuan, and the wanton behavior of
her brother Yang Guozhong.

In the scene *Tribute of Litchi*, Li Longji orders the use of a swift
horse to pay a tribute of litchi to Yang Yuhuan day and night from
the south. The scene is a direct reflection of national complaints.

Li Longji then takes Yang Yuhuan as his concubine, which was
not in line with the rules. He appoints crafty sycophants to cover
his personal affection, abandons state affairs, and even causes the
rebellion of An Lushan. Li Longji hastily evacuates from Chang'an,
but mutiny develops and the army officers ask the emperor to

get rid of the treacherous court official Yang Guozhong and his concubine. The emperor had no choice but order Yang Yuhuan to hang herself and their love has to be sublimated.

Yang Yuhuan misses Li Longji even after her death but Li Longji was disheartened and he passed the throne to the prince. He spent the rest of his life indulging his regret for losing his concubine without any relief.

Hong Sheng placed most of the emphasis on describing the twists and turns of the love between Li Longji and Yang Yuhuan. From their meeting to their increasing love, they made a secret vow to each other in the *Palace of Eternity* during the Double Seventh Festival, the legendary day in which lovers meet, to stay together forever.

It is a pity that this is not the ending of the touching story. Rebellion changes their relationship. Without any choice, Li Longji has to witness his lover leave him forever. A romantic love becomes a hopeless longing.

Yang Yuhuan and Li Longji were in the two different words. "Permanence, sometimes, comes to an end, while regret always finds no ending." This is an eternal tragedy.

Palace of Eternity is a great work. Through the confrontation and conflict between politics and love, the play places its characters, mainly Emperor Minghuang, in such an intensive confrontation that conciliation is impossible, and he has to reveal his inner embarrassment in face of the complicated contradiction.

The palace, with its numerous concubines, is an environment not conducive to sincere and pure love, but the love between Li Longji and Yang Yuhuan is that much more commendable because it grows in this extreme environment.

As an emperor, Li Longji has no way to protect his favorite concubine, but has to witness her death. His regret cannot be described in words.

Hong Sheng had outstanding literary talent. *Palace of Eternity* has a fairly high literary value and strict lyrics means the music layout closely matches the tunes.

Complicated plot and different characters need different styles of music, so that the music can match the scenes and characters. When the script came out, it was quickly staged and quickly became very popular because "whoever loves literature likes its lyrics, and whoever knows music likes its rhythms." It became the favorite play of scholars and gentlemen while actors competed to perform in it.

However, Hong Sheng and some of his friends suffered after the play came out, because performing *Palace of Eternity* before the end of the funeral period of Empress Tong, the mother of Emperor Kang Xi (reigned 1662–1722) was against the law. Many people were dismissed as punishment and Hong Sheng was expelled to his hometown. He drowned while drunk on his way to visit friends.

Another great play was *Peach Blossom Fan* (*Tao Hua Shan*), which along with the *Palace of Eternity*, was a great play of the early Qing Dynasty. It was written by Kong Shangren (1648–1718), who was born in Qufu, Shandong. Kong was among the 64th generation descendants of Confucius (551–479 BC).

Completed in the 38th year (1699) of Kang Xi, the play consists of 40 scenes, with four including an extra scene, for an actual total of 44.

During the late Ming Dynasty, with social unrest and the Li Zicheng (1606–1645) Uprising in particular, the army of the Qing Dynasty entered the Shanhaiguan Pass and the Ming Dynasty collapsed. From the uprising of starving people to the collapse of the Ming Dynasty and the founding of a new regime, a generation of scholars faced many tests of their core social values. The troubled times brought to an end their previous carefree life of song and dance, poems and wine. The change of dynasty forced a change in their lifestyle.

Having lived through the nation's troubles, Kong Shangren described the changing times by including current affairs into

A stage photo of Kunqu Opera *Peach Blossom Fan*, performed by Jiangsu Kunqu Troupe.

the play to show the connections between Hou Fangyu and other members of the Donglin Party and cunning official Ruan Dacheng.

In the beginning of the Qing Dynasty, the scholars in the south were still in strong conflict with the Qing court. Many well-known scholars were reluctant to serve as officials and rose against the Qing Dynasty one after another in various regions.

Kong Shangren wrote the play against this background. The theme and conception of the play reverberated with scholars and the people suffering from the collapse of the regime.

The play starts with a supporting role, a story-teller who describes how he sees the various characters. "Ah! How it made me weep, laugh, rage, even curse!"

This is the frame of mind of the various roles and audiences but also describes the author himself.

As the author described the play: "It used a romantic story of parting and reunion to relate the rise and fall of an empire"

showing a theme characteristic of *chuanqi* during the Ming and Qing.

Peach Blossom Fan inherited the characteristics of other *chuanqi* from the Ming and Qing dynasties that covered male and female roles in the lead that were skilled in expressing the love between men and women. The narration of the love between Hou Fangyu and Li Xiangjun, the hero and heroine of the play, reflects the tremendous changes caused by the change in the dynasties. The soft songs about the love between Hou Fangyu and Li Xiangjun love contrast with the dynastic changes. In the merry songs and graceful dances of scholars and singing girls, the play embodies the painful meaning of the story in the backdrop of the times.

The main story line of *Peach Blossom Fan* follows the love between scholar Hou Fangyu and singsong girl Li Xiangjun by the Qinhuai River. But the play has other, more complicated plot clues and numerous dramatic roles, with different characters and ambitions.

A stage photo of Kunqu Opera *Peach Blossom Fan*. The same fan witnessed the turns and twists of the hero and the heroine, and also the tremendous changes of the times, showing deep desolation in the alternation of sadness and joy.

Although Li Xiangjun was a singsong girl, she had more noble emotions than weak scholars. She refused to accept the gifts from Ruan Dacheng, a cunning and corrupt scholar, and encouraged Hou Fangyu to join the army to serve the nation. After Hou Fangyu joins the army and leaves, Ruan Dacheng forces Li Xiangjun to remarry to another man. She refuses, falls to the ground, and hits her head in an attempt to commit suicide; splattering her blood on the poem Hou Fangyu had given her when they first met. Hou Fangyu's friend Yang Longyou then uses the blood to paint a peach blossom on a fan. The poem fan with the peach blossom painted with the blood of Li Xiangjun's death shows how her ambitions become a symbol of determination.

The Southern Ming regime finally falls and Li Xiangjun becomes a nun. Hou Fangyu returns to look for her but, failing to find her, becomes a monk. Although they met again, their love is no longer.

Renouncing family is the desired end of Li and Hou, and also the end of the play.

Enlightened master Zhao Yaoxing reprimands Hou who still longed for Xiangjun: "When there are tremendous changes, you still indulge in love, it is really ridiculous!" "See, where you can find the nation, your family, you, and your father, but for this bit of love, can not you get rid of it?"

The idea of withdrawing from society and living in obscurity is not what the author wanted to advocate. What the end of the play represents is the sense of powerlessness reflected throughout the play. Knowing that the Ming Dynasty was doomed to fall, scholars were eager to serve the nation, but had no power to reverse time. Their great ambitions stood in great contrast with the reality that "scholars are useless" in difficult times. Therefore, what the play expresses is not a religious sentiment but a practical philosophy about the insignificance of scholars and people at a time when the state was coming to an end.

Peach Blossom Fan takes its time following the romances of various scholars with a hint of irony. Being simple and honest and unwilling to associate with cunning officials, scholars are really respectable, but unfortunately they have to work for the officials. In start contrast, after Hou Fangyu leaves, Li Xiangjun makes up her mind to insist on preserving her chastity for him. Having worked as a prostitute by the Qinhuai River, her vow chastity is a more staunch show of loyalty, as she becomes an example of moral integrity when the nation suffers a great catastrophe. Unfortunately, when compared with the fall of the emperor, the example is insignificant. The description, seemingly random, shows the author's pain at the fall of the state and the infinite memory and longing that exist beyond love.

Palace of Eternity and *Peach Blossom Fan* are two masterpieces from the early Qing Dynasty. Hong Sheng and Kong Shangren claimed their works were in strict accordance with historical facts and had no intentions to use baseless fabrication. Although they did not necessarily follow that strictly in creation, they exerted influence on the creation of a generation of plays.

Plenty of other tales from the Qing Dynasty took *Peach Blossom Fan* and *Palace of Eternity* as their basis, and were unavoidably subject to the seriousness and formality of the two plays.

At the time, operas based on fiction were criticized. The re-emergence of the odd conception like *Peony Pavilion* was unlikely. The decline of *chuanqi*, perhaps, was one of the causes.

Li Yu and Kunqu Opera Stage Performances

The rise of Kunqu Opera followed the performance system of *xiwen*. The types of roles used in *xiwen* during the Song and Yuan dynasties and in *zaju* of Yuan Dynasty were further differentiated and refined. The stage make-up, facial makeup and costumes followed more defined stereotypes. The combination of music and lyrics from Kunqu Opera promoted further standardization. The emergence of operas developed by common people changed its humble status.

Kunqu Opera performing artists came from all walks of life. The market-based development of opera spawned a large number of professional troupes while some scholars and officials set up family troupes to train performers, further promoting the move towards the refinement of Kunqu Opera and Chinese operas in general. These developments allowed for the mutual convergence of stage performances, scripts, and music from Kunqu Opera, elevating them all to an unsurpassed aesthetic peak. In just a few hundred years, Kunqu Opera incorporated traditional music, dance and literature, becoming the paramount example of Chinese culture.

From the Han, Tang, and Song dynasties to the Ming and Qing dynasties, China's opera performance venues can be divided into three categories. The first were halls in the palace as well as the residences of rich merchants and aristocracy. The second were performances in tile roofed houses and lower-grade open space by the road. The third were village temple stages in rural areas.

The performances in the palace and halls were identical in nature. Performers in these could be divided into two categories. Palace performances, such as those from educational institutions set up in the Han, Tang, and Song dynasties and those from family troupes run by scholars and aristocrats during the Ming and Qing dynasties. These performances targeted specific audiences. Performers had no commercial considerations and what was performed was actually up to the hosts. Performances put on in private residences, however, required higher quality.

During the Ming and Qing dynasties, social performances developed rapidly. These performances were staged in various venues, showing a gradual confluence with those in the palace and halls of aristocrats and nobles. The most common performances in these halls added a fair amount of fun to any feast. They started showing up in folk and commercial business premises and developed rapidly. Eventually, these performances became the mainstay of urban opera performances. As urban opera developed, people found more and more opportunities to appreciate operas.

It was on this wave of development emerging Suzhou playwrights like Li Yu (1591–1671), who were mostly lower and middle-class scholars living in the birthplace of Kunqu Opera. They had had the advantage of having a skilled command of Suzhou dialect phonology and could write plays for troupes that catered to the market-based evolution of Kunqu Opera in the area south of the Yangtze River centered on Suzhou.

Their scripts were tailored to the needs of opera performance. They were different from those written mainly for more well-known and higher-level scholars in aspects such as character relationships, setting and the use of language. They represented a new style of *chuanqi*.

Li Yu lived in the late Ming and early Qing dynasties. He was born in Wuxian, Jiangsu, into a humble family. Li Yu could not attend the imperial examination. Throughout the Qing Dynasty, he had no intention of seeking official rank and devoted all his life to research and the creation of opera.

His plays can be found in up to 42 different books of opera. Best known are his four masterpieces *Snow White Cup* (*Yi Peng Xue*), *Between Man and Beast* (*Ren Shou Guan*), *Forever Together* (*Yong Tuan Yuan*), and *Winning the Beauty Queen* (*Zhan Hua Kui*). All were very popular at that time. The four plays have been very common on Kunqu Opera stages.

One of Li's most outstanding plays, *Snow White Cup* includes 30 scenes. The name of the play originated from a legendary jade treasure from the Ming Dynasty. Wine in the cup would cool itself in summer without the help of ice and warm itself in winter without any fire. More strangely, when a good wine was poured, snowflakes would fly and mist float, so the cup was named "Snow White Cup."

The play tells the story of the cup, which is handed down from the ancestors of Mo Huaigu, a high official of the Court of Imperial Sacrifices. During the Jia Jing Period of the Ming Dynasty, Minister Yan Song and his son were domineering and unscrupulously plundered rare jade wares from around the world.

In the story, Yan and Mo are old family friends. Mo Huaigu recommended Tang Qin, his family's tutor skilled in antiques, to Yan Song's son Yan Shifan. However, Tang Qin returns good with evil and in order to curry the favor of Yan's family, and even attempt to grab Mo's wife Xueyan, he encourages Yan Shifan to take the jade cup by force from Mo Huaigu. Mo Huaigu tries to pass off a fake but Tang Qin sees through the ploy and Yan Shifan searches Mo's residence.

Mo Huaigu has to give up his rank and flee in panic but Yan's family eventually arrests him. Jizhou General Qi Jiguang is ordered to behead Mo Huaigu but Mo Cheng, a loyal servant of Mo's family, agrees to take his master's place and Mo Huaigu escapes.

The head of Mo Cheng is delivered to the capital but, again, Tang Qin sees through the ploy. Court guard Lu Bing is ordered to investigate with the help of Tang Qin. But Lu Bing discovers

Peking Opera *Snow White Cup*, Ma Changli plays the role of Mo Huaigu.

that Tang Qin had intended to grab Mo Huaigu's wife Xueyan.
With a hint from Xueyan, Lu Bing pretends to suspect that Xueyan
would be given to Tang Qin as a concubine. Tang Qin drops his
investigation and Xueyan pretends to accept that on face value but
uses the opportunity to kill Tang Qin and commits suicide after
taking revenge for Mo's family.

Xueyan then raises Mo Cheng's son Wenlu and Mo Huaigu
returns to Jinzhou. He meets his wife along with Wenlu offering a
sacrifice for him outside the west gate. The couple meet again and
take Wenlu as an adopted son and the family is reunited.

Snow White Cup has strong dramatic features and an evident
contrast between Tang Qing, who betrays his friend to seek
prosperity, and the humble servant Mo Cheng and the concubine
Xueyan. The touching image of Mo Cheng and Xueyan against
that of Tang Qin shows an insightful dramatic effect. Exciting and
attractive plots are quite interesting. Many scenes such as Trial of
Head and Killing Tang Qin are still performed on the stage and are
fairly popular.

Li Yu's plays *Snow White Cup*, *Forever Together*, *Between Man and Beast*, and *Winning the Beauty Queen* are based on common people. They focus on human sympathy and the reality of the time and meet the requirements for performance. Over time, performers sought to buy his plays and made Li Yu one of the earliest playwrights who could make a living writing plays.

After going into the Qing Dynasty, Li Yu's plays focused more on the political struggle or social life during the late Ming and early Qing. Among these plays were *Roster of the Loyal and Pure* (*Qing Zhong Pu*) and *Tragic Killing of Loyalists* (*Qian Zhong Lu*), both showed a higher level of dramatic creation.

The *Tragic Killing of Loyalists* describes how Zhu Di, prince of Yan, launched the Battle of Jingnan in the early Ming Dynasty. His army marches southward and turns the imperial capital of Nanjing into a sea of fire. Emperor Jianwen has to disguise himself as a monk and leave with the encouragement of the courtiers. He hurriedly leaves the capital but the loneliness of his escape and his anxiety from the unexpected turn of events can be seen in the following aria:

> *Put together the wonderful mountains and rivers, all the four elements are void. Having experienced a long journey, thick forests, high mountains, and the rolling waves of the Yangtze River... The country looks safe and sound, but who knows I alone came to Xiangyang with only a wooden ladle and a straw hat.*

Kunqu Opera during the Ming Dynasty included gorgeous lyrics and their themes focused on love and represented the pursuit of sultriness among scholars during the Ming Dynasty. They failed to express their more open minds. The emergence of Li Yu led to changes in *chuanqi* during the Ming Dynasty and infused more diverse masculine styles.

Many authors in the early Qing Dynasty left immortal works. Among them is *Story of Xiong Youlan and Xiong Youhui* (*Shuang*

Kunqu Opera *Tragic Killing of Loyalists*, Yu Zhenfei plays the role of Emperor Jianwen.

Xiong Meng) by Zhu Suchen.

Story of Xiong Youlan and Xiong Youhui, later known as *Fifteen Strings of Cash* (*Shi Wu Guan*), skillfully uses the double theme structure of the *chuanqi* classics of the Ming and Qing dynasties. The story focuses on how the brothers were involved in murder linked to 15 strings of bronze coins. A cunning official mistakenly judges the case and involves two innocent women. When the four people seem to be unavoidably heading towards punishment, righteous official Kuang Zhong finds flaws in the cases and carefully investigates despite a lot of pressure. He eventually arrests the murder and proves the four people to be innocent.

The play describes two unrelated pairs of men and women and two related cases. The structure is exquisite. The misfortunes of the four characters link them and the connections between life and death underscore the uncertainties of life.

In this era, the plays of Li Yu (1611–1680) are also worth mentioning. Among them are *Cherishing a Fragrant Companion* (*Lian Xiang Ban*), *A Wrong Kite* (*Feng Zheng Wu*), *Pavilion in the Mirage* (*Shen Zhong Lou*), and *Flatfish* (*Bi Mu Yu*). They were among the collection known as the 10 plays of Li Yu and were once very popular. Li Yu is one of the most important opera theorists in Chinese history. He wrote on and researched Kunqu Opera, he

A stage photo of Kunqu Opera *Fifteen Strings of Cash*.

taught family troupes to perform his plays, and handed down his devotion to script compilation, allowing the combination of Kunqu Opera performance and literature to reach new heights. His plays are mostly romantic stories. He did not dwell on profound thoughts or compassionate feelings, but he made his stories interesting and entertaining while fully tapping the elements of Kunqu Opera. He built a bridge between scholar elegance and other folk interests.

Promoted by scholars, the influence of Kunqu Opera is boundless and its music is quoted as official music by authorities. Actors are still subject to social discrimination, but the art of opera, on the whole, has jumped from the grassroots to the realm of elegant culture. The cultural significance of Kunqu Opera needs to be set in the even broader social vision that goes beyond the realm of opera to be fully understood and explained.

Flowers in Bloom: Diversified Opera Varieties

Spread of Yiyang Tune and Clapper Opera

Kunqu Opera won favor among middle and upper-class nobles and business people but in rural areas with relatively low economic development and levels of education, ornate diction and profound meaning did not necessarily arouse people's feeling. The exquisite productions of Kunqu Opera did not align well with the artistic orientation of folk opera performers.

From the Yuan Dynasty to the Ming Dynasty, folk operas entered a new stage of development and performances were held across the country. The emergence of rural opera performances created an opportunity for colorful forms to flourish and established a diversified pattern of Chinese opera.

Before the rise of Kunshan tune, Jiangsu and Zhejiang in the south of China witnessed the emergence of local tunes such as Haiyan tune, Yuyao tune and Yiyang tune. All were different from styles used in north China. Tunes, rhythm and even accompanying musical instruments fell into different musical systems and musicians from the south used them in operatic performances, formally opening a new diversified era of Chinese opera music. The

An ancient opera platform built in 1749 in Wuzheng, Zhejiang. There are such ancient opera platforms or theatres in various urban and rural areas around China.

later emergence of sophisticated and elegant Kunshan tune covered the brilliance of these systems but it did not completely replace them. In particular Yiyang tune, which was popular in the south, tied together with Kunqu Opera and spread to broader regions.

The process through which various local tunes in the south replaced northern *zaju* and became the most influential operatic form since the mid-Ming Dynasty underscored the joint progress of Kunqu, Yiyang tune and other styles. During the Ming and Qing dynasties, Kunqu Opera and Yiyang tune evolved together from the imperial to the public domains and were considered official and elegant music until the late Qing Dynasty. By contrast, folk tunes were considered to be merely presentable or acceptable for performance.

In fact, in the eyes of the literati, the fate of the Yiyang tune was different from Kunshan tune. After strict regulation by Wei Liangfu on rhythms of southern and northern operas, Kunshan tune rules made it easy to develop rhythm and create scripts. Further, the scripts were used to regulate and teach performers.

The spread of *chuanqi* scripts and Kunqu Opera led to a more enthusiastic and knowledgeable audience and curried the favor of scholars, which saw an increasingly upgraded aesthetic in Kunshan tune. Yiyang tune should have had the same position as Kunshan tune but a lack of masters like Wei Liangfu, who could develop rhythm rules, meant Yiyang tune evolved as it spread.

Yiyang tune rarely caught the attention of people and there are not many samples. However, a wide variety of high-pitched tune spread from south to

High-pitched tune
High-pitched tune is one of four classic tunes in Chinese traditional opera. The other three are Kunshan tune, Clapper tune and Pihuang tune. High-pitched tune is characterized by simple performances, popular lines and high-pitched singing with vocal accompaniment. Singers used only a gold drum, without orchestral accompaniment. From the mid-Ming Dynasty onwards, it began to spread from Jiangxi to the whole country. Different styles of high-pitched tune emerged across the country, including Hubei, Hunan, as well as Sichuan, Yunnan, Beijing and other provinces.

A stage photo of Sichuan Opera *Story of Burning Incense*.

north and can be considered a product of the convergence between Yiyang tune and local dialects and the music styles after Yiyang tune spread. Moreover, because Yiyang tune was unlike Kunshan tune and had no strict rules, the possibility for renovation increased significantly.

Unlike the slow and elegant Kunshan tune that could be sang softly and quietly, Yiyang tune had a rougher and straight music quality. The style of Yiyang tune that emerged naturally and spread widely included singing without orchestral instruments and vocal accompaniment to strengthen the opera performance. It relied largely on the strength of the natural voice to express dramatic emotions. This form of operatic music could, of course, maximize the vocal expression of emotion. The reason was that opera performances during the mid-Ming Dynasty were still in their early state, where vocal and instrumental music failed to be fully harmonized.

The storylines performed with Yiyang tune focused on loyalty, filial piety, integrity and righteousness coupled with impassioned and exciting music. Due to its extensive, rough, uninhibited and bright style, it was popular among the lower classes. In rural areas, operas were often staged in open-air temple stands with empty spaces and simple facilities. Rough folk opera forms with Yiyang tune as their representative were in line with the abilities of folk opera artists.

From the Song and Yuan dynasties, the general practice of opera performance was based on roughly fixed rules and forms of music, whether it was *xiwen*, *zaju* and Kunqu Opera. However, Yiyang tune spread among ordinary people and did not follow strict rules. It allowed folk artists to create freely.

From the mid-Ming Dynasty, Yiyang tune changed to varying degrees as it spread. As it spread, there were incremental changes in what were originally fixed scripts, breaking the connecting mechanism and gradually enhancing the impression that opera music was based on the expansion and renovation of scripts. There were many varieties that evolved into a complicated system of high-pitched tunes.

However, operas with significant local styles sprang up in the south and north, marking the beginning of the local era of Chinese opera. Local operas increasingly demonstrated their importance

A stage photo of Shaanxi Opera *Yang Qiniang*.

Quanshan aria

Quanshan aria is the most common folk ditty in the central Shaanxi plain. It was most commonly used in Taoism to advocate doctrines at means of temple fairs and folk events during the Ming and Qing dynasties. Taoist *quanshan* aria can be seen to this day. Content mainly covers moral enlightenment. Stories like *Twenty-four Stories about Filial Piety* had lyrics following the seven and ten-character line structure.

and became the mainstay of local performances. Yiyang tune had significant influence on dozens of operas and became an important part of the development of Chinese folk opera.

It is not clear how Yiyang tune spread to various regions but the distribution of operas with high-pitched tunes is enough to show the scope of the spread. Indeed, the process of the style's spread matched the process of renovation by folk artists. The style was incorporated into various local styles and became the basis for a wide range of local tunes.

The emergence of Shaanxi Opera in northwest part of China was another important segment of the tune art development of Chinese opera.

Shaanxi Opera emerged in the central Shaanxi plain. Its main aria was based on the *quanshan* aria popular in the location. The major style of Kunqu Opera and high-pitched tunes is *qupai*, which had different length of long and short lines but relatively strict rules.

Shaanxi Opera was a new style. Lyrics can be classified into two types: Lines with seven Chinese characters and lines with ten. A music unit consists of two lines with the same number of characters, which consists of the same number of words, and can be called couplets, which are the most common style of various local operas.

Shaanxi Opera has a long history. In the *Lotus in Earthen Bowl* (*Bo Zhong Lian*), a recently discovered opera performed in the south during the Wanli Period (1573–1620) of the Ming Dynasty, there is a section which uses couplets of seven or ten-character lines.

Shaanxi Opera launched a brand new style of music to sing in Chinese opera. It was generally known as the *banqiang* style. *Banqiang* was the most common music form of local opera. The well-known Hanju Opera, Peking Opera, Cantonese Opera and Shaoxing Opera, Pingju Opera and Huangmei Opera familiar to people are all based on the *banqiang* style. With simple structures and distinct rhythms, *banqiang* style is easy to master and suitable for folk opera performances. Seemingly simple, the *banqiang* style implies the possibility of many changes due to its simple lyrics.

Although Shaanxi Opera takes the two-six-beats style from quanshan aria as its basic means of singing, it still retained quite a few tunes. However, these tunes are generally not suitable for singing and many are used before the opening, during the interlude or through the performance to render or accentuate the mood.

In the process of formation of Shaanxi Opera, a clapper-based instrumental accompaniment system emerged. By the mid-Qing Dynasty, percussion music gradually evolved based on drumbeats and supplemented by such metal instruments as cymbals and gongs, leading to the special gong and drum ensemble. Before a

Shaanxi Opera performance in village is popular and vital

Shaanxi Opera performance, opening drums and gongs were used as the prelude to create a heated and warm atmosphere, especially in open-air venues and became a way to attract large audiences before a performance.

During a performance, different gong and drum ensembles are used in different opera scenarios and each has a special effect on creating the right atmosphere. Clappers with individual characteristics control the performance and accompany the band and the leader of the band directs the music with clappers, so Shaanxi Opera is also known as clapper opera.

As an independent and mature style, Shaanxi Opera spread around the country. The spread of Shaanxi Opera benefited partly from the Li Zicheng Uprising. Li Zicheng led the uprising in 1629 and finally took Beijing in 1644, overthrowing the Ming.

Farmers turned soldiers in Shaanxi were the mainstay of the Li Zicheng troops, which were said to have taken Shaanxi Opera as their troop music, so many Shaanxi Opera performers joined them. Whenever they went, they would celebrate big victories with Shaanxi Opera performance at the local Temple of Guan Yu. After defeats, Shaanxi Opera performers along with the troops would scatter, enabling the rapid spread of Shaanxi Opera. As the style spread, it combined with local music forms to create new styles of clapper opera and gained a presence around the country to form huge families of clapper operas.

Like the high-pitched tune system, Shaanxi Opera is completely different from Kunqu Opera in style orientation, and has musical characteristic that are easily accepted by ordinary people. As a result, this style became highly influential during the Ming and Qing dynasties.

The characters and plots of Kunqu Opera focus more on the performance of *sheng* (the male role) and *dan* (any female role). Love stories are the most common. Shaanxi Opera, with its grassroots base, was quite different from Kunqu Opera even if the most popular theme is also the expression of love.

Famous Shaanxi Opera artist Wei Changsheng (1744–1802) came to Beijing to perform *Wallowing on the Floor* (*Gun Lou*) in 1779. In the opera, he plays a girl who opposes the court and becomes a bandit. One night, she sleeps in the same room with Wang Ziying, a defeated general. The man and the woman love each other and promise each other marriage. They are married on the spot pursuant to the traditional Chinese marriage ceremony.

Wei Changsheng used graceful body language and charming expressions to fully show the forcefulness in both love and hate of the leading female role but also a sort of emotional shyness. Wei's bold, delicate and provocative performance was moving. Wei lifted Shaanxi Opera performances to a new realm and this emerging style a popular among Beijing audiences. Artists in various regions then copied his style.

Competition between *Huabu* and *Yabu*

Various local tunes thrived during the Qing Dynasty and challenged Kunqu Opera that only advocated mainstream culture.

Peking Opera *Anhui Opera Troupes Come to Beijing*, shows the grand event of four major Anhui Opera troupes' Beijing tour in the Qing Dynasty.

A three-storied theatrical stage in the Forbidden City in Beijing

Yangzhou, a very important commercial port near Suzhou, witnessed the gathering of Huizhou merchants while a tour by Emperor Qianlong's (1736–1795) stimulated the prosperity of opera performances. The result was something of a local competition between *huabu* and *yabu*.

Yabu was the performance of Kunqu Opera while *huabu* included Shaanxi Operas, Yiyang tune, Clapper Opera, Luoluo tune and Erhuang melody, showing the co-existence of diversified tune patterns in Chinese operas.

Local tune patterns, called *huabu* during the Qing Dynasty, sprang up, and increasingly became major types of operas for local performances. In *huabu*, also known as *luantan*, the most important and influential style is Peking Opera.

The rise of Peking Opera was linked to the Yangzhou Salt Administrative Organ. In the 55th year (1790) of Emperor Qianlong, the imperial government took local troupes to come to perform in Beijing to celebrate the emperor's birthday. The Huizhou opera troupe from Yangzhou was the most popular. The top four Huizhou opera troupes formed in Beijing performed operas with diversified tune patterns including Kunqu Opera, Clapper Opera, and Erhuang melody. Their colorful performances gradually won the favor of audiences in Beijing and the imperial capital's opera performance scene become increasingly active.

At the same time, thanks to performances of Hanju Opera (popular along the Yangtze River and Hanshui River drainage areas within Hubei) emerged alongside Huizhou opera troupes in Beijing. Hanju and Huizhou opera troupes complemented each other. The result was Peking Opera, which soon become one of the most popular types of operas.

Peking Opera is intrinsically compatible with Beijing's culture in terms of theme, singing style and unique performance system. It emerged in Beijing as a result of a mixing of numerous types of operas.

The growth and development of Peking Opera were closely related with imperial court opera performances. The Qing Dynasty set up special organs and employed folk trainers to teach eunuchs to perform Kunqu Opera and Yiyang tune opera for emperors. After the mid-Qing Dynasty, empress fond of operas invited performers to perform in the imperial palace so as to meet their needs for opera appreciation. Starting from the reign of Emperor Guangxu, a large number of troupes were invited to perform in the palace and recruited famous performers to stage in the palace on occasions not limited to birthday celebration and grand ceremonies. The opera performances were based on *luantan*.

Tea house

The tea house was a typical venue for opera performances in Beijing during the late Qing Dynasty. The core facility of tea house was the stage along the side of which there were tables. Tea and snacks were available. The major function of tea house was the opera performance. Although guest expenses were typically called payment for tea, the enjoyment of the performances was the primary attraction. The payment for tea varied from seat to seat, depending on the location and the ability to see the performance. Tea houses also had some social functions. One side of tea house was a square stage with three open sides.

The theatrical stage in the residence of Prince Gong of Qing Dynasty built in 1777.

Portraits of Peking Opera characters played by famous actors of late Qing Dynasty, painted by Shen Rongpu, a well-known portraitist active in the late Qing period.

For outstanding Peking Opera performing artists outside the palace, Empress Dowager Cixi and Ci'an, Emperor Guangxu (reigned 1875–1908) and others would give rich rewards after performances. Folk trainers, originally employed to teach eunuchs, gradually took performance as their major function.

The growth of opera as a common hobby among ordinary people was an even more important impetus to the development of Peking Opera. During the Qing Dynasty, tea houses that provided Peking Opera performance emerged rapidly in Beijing. As the demand for performances grew, so did the number of troupes. These troupes were often led by a well-known actor supplemented by other supporting roles during performance, like well-known Peking Opera male performers Cheng Changgeng (1811–1880), Yu Sansheng (1802–1866), and Zhang Erkui (1814–1860).

Peking Opera inherited rich and diversified operas. Chinese operas evolved from story-telling from the Tang and Song dynasties and were later closely related with folk storytelling to the accompaniment of stringed instruments. Romance of *Three Kingdoms* (*San Guo Yan Yi*), *Outlaws of the Marsh* (*Shui Hu Zhuan*), *Investiture of the Gods* (*Feng Shen Bang*) and *Flying-dragon's Biography*

(*Fei Long Zhuan*) were all adapted into a large number of opera performances. History expressed in popular folk stories offered numerous elements that could be directly changed into the stories that could be staged and constituted the core theme of Chinese operas. Significantly different from Kunqu Opera over-indulging in scholar and love stories, Peking Opera covered such themes as the sense of national identity, legal cases, devils and love stories, in particular, heroic legends deriving from story-telling were very popular.

Indeed, Peking Opera inherited lots of important operas from Kunqu Opera, but even more from Clapper Opera and other such styles that were more suitable for common people and to entertain audiences in theaters. This common attraction made Peking Opera different from Kunqu Opera in its performance style and further promoted the development and performance level of Peking Opera.

The special performing system of Peking Opera played a positive role in improving the maturity and performance level of the opera. Focusing on performing opera highlights, Peking Opera was quite different from the common performing systems of other styles.

Tan Xinpei plays the role of Yang Yanhui in *The Fourth Son of the Yang Family Visits His Mother.*   Tan Xinpei in real life.

Xiwen during the Song and Yuan dynasties and *zaju* during Yuan Dynasty formed complete opera play systems, marking a stage of maturity for Chinese opera. A play lasted between three to six hours or longer and performance of a whole play spoke of an inherent integrity. This was the care particularly with Peking Opera, which inherited the performing system of Kunqu Opera and focused on opera highlights from the very beginning of its formation. Whether performed in the palace or outside, in the afternoon or in the evening, a theater would stage five or six to more than ten opera highlights in a row rather than a big opera play during a certain period of time.

The rapid development of Peking Opera was also attributable to some renowned performing artists such as Cheng Changgeng and Tan Xinpei (1847–1917).

Tan Xinpei was one of the greatest performing artists in the history of Peking Opera. Among the numerous classic Peking Opera plays, he fully demonstrated his unique tune with a rather desolate sense and shaped many desperately tragic heroes. His most famous play, *The Battle of Dingjunshan* (*Ding Jun Shan*), as well as other plays such as *Qin Qiong Selling His Horse* (*Qin Qiong Mai*

Ma), *Story of Black Pot* (*Wu Pen Ji*), *A Child Left in the Mulberry Garden* (*Sang Yuan Ji Zi*), and *The fourth Son of the Yang Family Visits His Mother* (*Si Lang Tan Mu*) created enthusiasm among the audience for the plays showed the plights and minds of unappreciated heroes. He found a compassionate voice with special feelings to perform such tragic figures rare in the history of opera. He was good at performing not the high-spirited moments of these heroes, but deliberately showed the most dismal experiences of their lives with his special and sort of rough voice and tunes on the stage.

The most representative was the hero Qin Qiong who had great talent but was forced to sell his favorite war horse. Time and again he repeats the value of his horse with complicated emotions, and lastly just shakes his head: "Just take it to your home, but I am not sure where it will settle down." With mild Tan's voice to show Qin Qiong's frustration, his performance contributed to Peking Opera, and also one of the most characteristic aspects of Chinese operas.

At the time of Tan Xinpei popularity, his classic arias had a unique style earning this era it's a unique aesthetic tag. Tan Xinpei's performance showed the essence of traditional aesthetics: Complaining without anger and sadness without hurt, overflowing with unique sense of decadence and the vicissitudes of home and nation; a millennium-old empire's last legs were shown in front of people with more vividly manifested voice of Tan Xinpei than anything else.

The product of the competition between *huabu* and *yabu* was the emergence of Peking Opera that was enough to replace the cultural position of Kunqu Opera.

Meanwhile, in China's other regions such as Hubei, Sichuan, Jiangsu and Zhejiang as well as neighboring Fujian along the Yangtze River drainage, Shanxi, Henan, and Shandong in North China, the spread of high-pitched tunes and *luantan* spawned a large number of operas with local tunes. Some important ones were Shanxi Opera, Henan Opera, Hebei Clapper Opera, and Shandong Laizhou Clapper Opera, Cantonese Opera, Fujian Opera, Jiangxi

Opera, and Sichuan Opera. The emergence of new operas inspired a new upsurge in the development of Chinese opera.

From Playlet to Big Opera

During the Han and Tang dynasties, early opera performances fell into two categories: *ta-yao-niang* and *canjun* opera.

Folk songs and dances widely distributed throughout various regions in the south and north emerged as a natural extension of the *ta-yao-niang* style song and dance performances. Due to geographical differences, they were called flower-drum opera, flower-lantern opera, tea-picking opera, and *yangge* opera etc. These performances were often seen at festival celebrations and temple festivals, and their origin was associated with folk beliefs but, as they evolved, their entertainment quality grew. The content of folk songs and dances was mostly small stories with interesting and emotional performances by male and female singers and dancers complemented by distinctive local ditties. Having spread for many years, these folk songs and dances rose in rural areas with similar performances although they were prohibited by feudal

The photo describes the actual scene of Peking Opera performance in a tea house of the Qing Dynasty.

officials.

Around 1900, Huangxiao flower-drum opera (popular in Hubei's Huangban and Xiaogan) artists began to enter Wuhan, a large city along the middle reaches of the Yangtze River, and performed relatively complete plays in some regular tea houses in towns. The originally unpopular performances were rooted in Wuhan but in a short period of a little more than ten years they became a new and fairly popular opera style—Chuju Opera.

Huangxiao Flower-drum Opera is a typical example of playlet that included various local song and dance performances. Its performance includes a simple plot with a male role and a female role—which is often called a two-role playlet. The performances focused more on folk love stories, for example, *12-month Longing* (*Shi Er Xiang*), which describes how the woman Zhang Erjie longs for Yu Laosi. Then Yu Laosi emerges on the stage. From the first lunar month to the twelfth lunar month, Zhang and Yu sing in turn. During the performance, a bamboo curtain is used to separate them, meaning that they are in two different places. They long for each other and complaint about each other, showing both deep love and humor.

These small plays gradually developed towards a more dramatic orientation. For instance, *Aunt Wang Asking after Zhang Erjie* (*Wang Da Niang Wen Bing*), also called *Outside the Window Screen* (*Sha Chuang Wai*). In the play, there are two roles—Aunt Wang and Zhang Erjie. Zhang is ill and Wang comes to look after her. Wang asks about the cause of her illness and Zhang answers in various arias. Eventually, Zhang narrates the source of her illness, which is related to her longing for a scholar.

Two-role playlet and three-role playlet

Xiwen during Song and Yuan dynasties and *zaju* of Yuan Dynasty included many roles. However, at the same time, there were more small folk songs and dances as well as story-telling performances. With some dramatic features, the performances focused on two-role antiphonal singing and were known as two-role playlet with antiphonal singing by a young male role and a young female role, or by a clown and a young female role. At times there was a third role, which became the element that adjusted the atmosphere and created a more dramatic space between the two main roles and became known as the three-role playlet performed by a young male role, a young female role and a clown. Both two-role and three-role playlets share some common features. Their musical forms roughly correspond to the lyrics with two couplets of lines. Their backbone rhythms are generally simple and easy to remember and sing. Complicated techniques are not required. These playlets spread quickly and many new operas evolved from them.

Flower-drum opera *Selling Groceries* is a typical two-role playlet.

The playlet developed into a flower-drum opera — *Wu Sanbao's Spring Sightseeing* (*Wu San Bao You Chun*) in which the heroine was Zhao Saihua. Zhao meets Wu Sanbao during spring sightseeing. Wu deliberately loses his white fan and Zhao picks it up and returns home with great longing and becomes ill. Aunt Wang witnesses the events and goes to Zhao's to look after her, promising to match the couple. Meanwhile, Wu is also sick and Aunt Wang goes to look after him, knowing of their mutual love. Aunt Wang asks them to her home to help them achieve their long-cherished wish.

Because it evolved from folk songs and dances, Huangxiao flower-drum opera still maintained a style that focused on folk antiphonal singing between a man and a woman long after it spread in cities. Its lyrics and content showed distinct folk styles, using bold and direct expressions of passion and vivid lyrics coupled with widespread simple and pleasant folk music. It quickly won most audiences and enriched the content of Chinese operas.

In the early 20th century, folk storytelling and singing in the vicinity of Shanghai also began to evolve towards operas, marking the birth of many new works.

Tanhuang, a form of story-telling in south of the Yangtze River, was story-telling accompanied by drum lyrics. It emerged following opera scripts from the Song Dynasty. *Tanhuang* was first performed in tea houses with easily understandable lyrics. It often focused on boudoir scandals, so it was often prohibited by feudal officials and criticized by scholars. In the early 20th century, some *tanhuang* artists staged playlets that ranged from simple men and women performers without make-up to stage performances with dramatic roles. *Tanhuang* in the vicinity of Changzhou and Wuxi thus developed and became a new opera form known as Wuxi Opera.

The most influential traditional play of Wuxi Opera was *Meet in the Temple* (*An Tang Xiang Hui*), which was originally a very popular *tanhuang* in the vicinity of Wuxi during the late Qing Dynasty. The play describes how the heroine Jin Xiuying had been betrothed from childhood to Chen Axing, who lived in the same village. Jin grew up with her fiancé Chen, but times changed. Jin's family became rich while Chen's family declined. Her father attempted to repudiate the marriage contract but Jin went to meet Chen in secret.

The lyrics of the *tanhuang* spoke about the poverty of Chen's family: "Your are the clay Buddha statute that cannot be raised, rush lamp wick that cannot be straightened, decayed bean curd that cannot be picked up, and leather rope that cannot be cooked well. You are the cooker that cannot be heated even for a hundred days, and the stone mill whose core has decayed for a thousand years. You are like a dead person just with a more breath, and just like a rotten woodcarving." The lyrics are full of vivid and quite wonderful metaphors.

Tanhuang prevailed in the vicinity of Jiangsu and Zhejiang during the late Qing Dynasty. The local *tanhuang*, called Dongxiang tune near Shanghai, grew from a small sitting singing of three to five people and changed from simple sitting and singing into singing while playing a role. The performances caught the attention of audiences day after day in tea houses and story-telling venues in Shanghai and nearby towns.

In the tea houses in Shanghai, such performances were fairly popular, and gradually evolved towards opera. The tune pattern

A stage photo of Chuju Opera *Broken Bridge*, set in folk tale *Legend of White Snake*, is mainly about the love story between white snake spirit and scholar Xu Xian.

was complemented with some ordinary ditties based on the originally simple long tunes and beats of story-telling *tanhuang* tunes. Melodies and rhythms changed gradually and became increasingly diversified, and eventually formed a new opera, Shanghai Opera. Examples like *Meeting in the Temple, A Bida Going Home (A Bi Da Hui Niang Jia), Lu Yachen, Qiuxiang Delivers Tea (Qiu Xiang Song Cha)*, and *Grinding Soybean to Make Bean Curd (Mo Dou Fu)*, these were often performed after such local *tanhuang* developed and became Shanghai Opera.

Shaoxing Opera originating from Zhejiang developed even more rapidly.

Shaoxing Opera emerged from *tanhuang* story-telling and singing that was long popular in Zhejiang's Shengxian County and surrounding rural areas. During the Ming and Qing dynasties, artists performed *tanhuang* to make a living. Performers developed songs and unique performances by changing purely story-singing into an early form of performance with both singing and story-telling, forming relatively complete stories and music with a uniform style. They were good at singing the stories that had been known for a long time, many of which derived from folk narratives such as *Pearl Pagoda* (*Zhen Zhu Ta*), *Story of Selling Wife* (*Mai Po Ji*), and *Selling Charcoal* (*Mai Qing Tan*). Most of these scripts could be played for several days and even a few months, and they later became the rudiment of scripts of Shaoxing Opera, and are performed even to this day.

In the process of performance, basic musical structures with smooth and pleasant rhythms and melodies took shape while the quality of the performances increased constantly. In the Spring Festival in 1906, some performers in Shengxian County staged their performances of various roles with make-up in Yuhang and Lin'an in Zhejiang and other places at the request of wealthy families and villagers, marking the significant transformation from story-singing to stage performance. As they did not rely on orchestral instruments when singing and just used a ring-stiffened drum and a pair of rosewood boards to produce the sound of *didu*, these groups were called *didu* troupes. On the basis of the *didu* troupes, a new opera, Shaoxing Opera emerged.

In the Spring Festival of 1938, Yao Shuijuan (1916–1976) led her Shaoxing Opera troupe with all female performers to Shanghai, marking a new and important chapter in the history of Shaoxing Opera.

Although Yao was an actress, she was good at playing male roles. At the time, Shaoxing Opera troupes with all woman performers were common and developed a unique aesthetic style, wining the favor of numerous audiences in Jiangsu and Zhejiang, with growing professional training of women performers of Shaoxing Opera.

Shaoxing Opera with women performers is known for its soft tunes and rhythms full of sadness and pathos. It features the habits of people in Shanghai while retaining the purity from villages as well as a clear and elegant folk singing style. Shaoxing Opera inherited a large number of plays and common issues to cater to people migrating from different regions to Shanghai. It gradually changed its style and improved its artistic content according to the new needs of residents.

The tune pattern and music style of Shaoxing Opera embodies the feminine style of the beautiful landscapes in the south of the Yangtze River. The male roles played by female performers further reinforce this feminine style. For the same beautiful love story, it can better show the emotional turns and twists; for the same miserable life tragedy, it is more appropriate to express sadness.

In Shaoxing Opera performances, female performers of young male roles create a its unique enchantment. Following Yao Shuijuan, Yin Guifang (1919–2000) displayed the characteristics of Shaoxing Opera with women performers. With traditional opera plays *He Wenxiu* and *Prince of Desert* (*Sha Mo Wang Zi*) which adapted from the US film *Cabin in the Sky* and hundreds of other plays, Yin established her position in the realm of Shaoxing Opera

Shaoxing Opera *Fortune-telling* from *He Wenxiu*.

A stage photo of *Dream of the Red Chamber*, a classical Shaoxing Opera play.

and displayed the enchantment of female performers of young male roles to the maximum.

He Wenxiu is a traditional play of Cantonese Opera. A scholar named *He Wenxiu* is victimized by a treacherous feudal official named Yan Song and He's whole family suffered from the misfortune. Only He Wenxiu escapes to make a living by singing opera. Wang Lanying, a girl from a rich family learns of this bad experience and finds him both good-looking and talented. The two meet in private and are married but their marriage is not accepted by Wang's family. The couple flees to Haining. Unexpectedly, Zhang Tang, the richest local man, makes a false charge against them and the two are forced to separate. He flees again, while Wang is saved by Aunt Yang, a tea house owner. The more exciting parts of the story are in *Visiting His Wife in Mulberry Garden* (*Sang Yuan Fang Qi*) and *Fortune-telling* (*Suan Ming*). He Wenxiu is saved and escapes a second time. He inquires into his wife's residence. Coincidentally, his wife was holding the third-year memorial ceremony for him. But Zhang Tang was still in the picture and He

Yin Guifang, known as the Emperor of Shaoxing Opera, is guiding a rehearsal. Teaching by personal example as well as verbal instruction has long been a unique way of inheritance of Chinese operas.

fears being discovered, so he dressed up as a fortune teller and visits his wife. At Yang's home, Wang asks the fortune-teller to tell the fortune of her husband. He, holding an abacus, pretends to be calm but his grief grows: "Specific birthday is distinct. Wenxiu will tell his own fortune. I cannot tell the fortune of others, but can tell mine accurately."

Yao Shuijuan to Yin Guifang pioneered women's Shaoxing Opera. In subsequent years, audiences fully accepted Shaoxing Opera plays by all female performers, and the style has rapidly become the most popular in the city. Decades later, Shaoxing Opera is performed all over the country, and there are numerous fans of the opera in a wide range of regions.

From the late 19th century to the early 20th century, performing artists in Hebei turned their talking and singing performances into

Pingju Opera.

Lianhualao and *yangge*, performed in the rural areas of Hebei and Tianjin, were commonly known as *laozi* and *bengbeng*. They were previously favorite songs, dances and ditties of local people and there were often folk artists who attempted to stage their performances. The desire to stage *laozi* performances enabled *laozi* performers in the early 20th century to gradually set up many troupes, most of which were made up of seven or eight people. They

Portrait of Cheng Zhaocai.

came to Tianjin in succession. The region under the jurisdiction of the Qing government had strict control over *laozi*, so the troupes would often select the tea houses in the concession and some uncontrolled areas to perform or they would make enclosures for open air performances.

Their performances covered increasingly rich contents and plots and the genre also changed from narration to prosopopeia style. In turn, the different roles, costume and make-up changed towards diversification from previous clowns with wrapped forehead and pigtails along with some simple colors coated on face. *Little Miss Chatterbox* (*Xiao Gu Xian*) and *Picking Plum Branches* (*Shi Mei Zhi*) all have become independent and can be performed with make-up. While simple and rough, these performances boast strong entertainment features and are therefore are very popular.

In 1909, the nascent Pingju Opera entered Tangshan, a core city in the eastern part of Hebei. It showed extraordinary appeal in highly commercialized competition and matured quickly. Early Pingju Opera artists, Wang Fengting and Cheng Zhaocai (1874–1929) et al selected opera topics from such works as *Wonders of the Present and the Past* (*Jin Gu Chuan Qi*) and staged such performances

Pingju Opera *Third Sister Yang Goes to Court*, Xin Fengxia plays the role of the Third Sister Yang.

as *Flower is a Go-between* (*Hua Wei Mei*), *Widow Named Ma Sets up a Store* (*Ma Gua Fu Kai Dian*), and *Winning the Beauty Queen* (*Zhan Hua Kui*). With successful performances, the quality of Pingju Opera improved substantially and performers made comprehensive and systematic renovations of *lianhualao* through such aspects roles, tune patterns, movement and accompaniment, laying an artistic foundation.

Cheng Zhaocai played a vital role in the development of Pingju Opera. He was one of the key figures in the process of the transition of Pingju Opera from *lianhualao* to Tangshan *laozi* performed on the stage. The most important was that he laid the opera play foundation for Pingju Opera through his constant creation. Even to this day, where Pingju Opera is performed, people can still enjoy Cheng's works. The plays he created backed up Pingju Opera, making Pingju Opera one of the most influential operas in the vast North and Northeast China.

Cheng left no less than 90 Pingju Opera plays. *Third Sister Yang Goes to Court* (*Yang San Jie Gao Zhuang*), based on the situation of his time, was an outstanding representative. It was long performed on the stage. *Third Sister Yang Goes to Court* was based on a real event that happened in Luanxian County, Hebei, in 1918. Since its debut in 1919, the performance of the play has not ceased. The story was that the third sister Yang, a peasant girl, accused the family of her brother-in-law of killing her second elder sister. She goes to the county government office to complain but the officials were involved in bribery and graft. Yang then goes to the Tianjin Higher Procuratorial Department to appeal and the case is finally approved by the newly appointed director general. The coffin of her sister is opened to inspect the body and the truth is discovered and the murderer executed. The story shows the struggle of a woman at the bottom of the society who fights against the tyranny of the rich and powerful. Yang's perseverance inspired numerous audiences.

The emergence of Chuju Opera, Shaoxing Opera, Pingju Opera and other operas had a special significance in the development process of Chinese opera. Generally speaking, the predecessors of these operas can be divided into two categories.

One category, for example, flower-drum opera, lantern opera, tea-picking opera, and *yangge*, evolved from folk songs and dances. They show simple performing methods—singing over dancing, and some small plays are based on certain stories, often involving mutual longing, flirtation, and love between a man and a woman. Occasionally there are some satires on greediness, meanness and laziness, mainly for fun. From simple songs and dances to the performances of some small stories, the performing methods diversified toward playing and simulating roles in plays, marking the key segment for the transformation of songs and dances to opera performance. These initially formed small plays are based mostly on well-known local folk tales, constituting the original narrative tradition of various new operas.

Another category evolved from talking and singing, for example, the operas derived from *lianhualao, tanhuang,* and *daoqing* popular from the south to the north. A clear distinction between then and singing and dancing is that they also have some short plays, but they have the tradition of telling long stories.

Starting from the Tang and Song dynasties, the style prevailed until its transition from temples to folk performances and became a type of popular entertainment performance.

Yangliuqing New Year Picture *Shibuxian*. *Shibuxian* was a folk art popular in Beijing, Tianjin, and Hebei during the Qing Dynasty with contents mostly covering folk stories accompanied by 10 percussion instruments such as gongs, drums, cymbals, and reverse cymbals.

Between talking and singing and operas, there is obvious difference. Talking and singing is narrative, while opera is prosopopeia style. And another distinction is whether performers are in costume. But just as the initial operas during the Song and Yuan dynasties were closely related with talking and singing, China has a tradition that talking and singing are staged to become operas, not only due to the relationship between the verse of talking and singing and prose, which facilitates the transformation of the script into to opera plays, and the vividness of performances is similar to that of operas. Of course, talking and singing are performed by two performers together while opera requires more roles. For talking and singing, a man and a woman perform alternately, but the libretto is general, and performers are mostly familiar with each other. Several groups of performers wear make-up and play different roles, so performing a play is easy for them. As for the performance level, it naturally needs constant improvement.

Singing and dancing as well talking and singing are full of folk styles for they were popular among the people at the bottom of society. They are particularly appropriate for stories of the family loves but not for such topics as politics and military. They are short, so they are commonly known as playlets.

In just a few decades, various regions around China witnessed the emergence of Huangmei Opera, Hunan Flower-drum Opera, Jiangxi Tea-picking Opera, Yunnan Lantern Opera, and Shandong Lüju Opera, as well as new operas transformed from *yangge* and *daoqing* in the north of China, which, to varying degrees, absorbed the advantages of such big operas as Kunqu Opera, high-pitched tunes, and *luantan*, and whose plays, music and performance became diversified. At the same time, they continued to maintain the characteristics of interesting and humorous lyrics and performance styles and embody the wisdom and imagination of the grassroots so they became very popular. After the 1920s, their rise was unstoppable.

Modern Play and Stage Play

In the late 19th century, cultural exchanges between China and the western world became increasingly close and dramas originating in Europe were introduced into China, adding a new landscape to Chinese operas.

Shanghai, opened first as a commercial port in China, was the birthplace of Chinese operas. In the mid-19th century, an increasing number of expatriates from various western countries gathered in Shanghai and brought Western dramas to China. Westerners built and run churches and schools, which created opportunities for dramas to enter China.

Shanghai's first drama performance can be traced back to 1850 when the Amateur Dramatic Troupe was set up in the British Concession. The Amateur Dramatic Club of Shanghai (ADC) set up by western expatriates living in Shanghai in 1866 staged western classic drama plays in the decades that followed. In 1874, Shanghai Lyceum Theater was completed, becoming the fixed performance venue of ADC in the concession.

The dramas at that time were performed in the special theaters in the concessions. The performers and staff were western expatriates, using western languages, rehearsing western plays and the audience was basically foreign expatriates.

Later, westerns in the concession ran mission schools, for example, French-run College St. lgnace organized students to produce religious every year. The form of the performance was different from traditional singing alternated with monologue, marking the first contact for Chinese people with performing drama.

Liturgical drama inspired mission school students' interest in drama creation and performance. In 1889, the students of John's College, a mission school in Shanghai, performed *A Scandal in the Officialdom* (*Guan Chang Chou Shi*), opening the beginning of China's modern drama creation based on current affairs. The custom of students' drama performance had influence on western-style schools run by Chinese people.

In 1900, Shanghai Nanyang College students staged *Six Gentlemen* (*Liu Jun Zi*), *On the Nation* (*Jing Guo Mei Tan*), and *Boxer Uprising* (*Yi He Tuan*)—three modern dramas on current affairs. Nanyang College and Beiyang University were the universities first run by the Chinese people in modern history.

The fact that groups of Chinese students rehearsed and staged such drams using ways different from traditional operas makes it certain that western-style had really extended their presence to China.

In the early 20th century in Shanghai, drama performances by students quickly prevailed. In 1903, Yucai School performed *Zhang Wenxiang Assassinated Ma Xinyi* (*Zhang Wen Xiang Ci Ma*). In the play, Ma Xinyi, general governor of Jiangsu and Jiangxi and a provincial magnate, is killed by assassin Zhang Wenxiang. The case

A stage photo of *Black Slaves' Appeal to Heaven*, performed by Chunyang Society in 1907.

shocks the court and the people. The complicated causes, especially the identity of the assassin Zhang Wenxiang who was a remnant of the Taiping Heavenly Kingdom stimulated people's imagination. Rumors spread. Even before the case was concluded, the Shanghai Opera House had already compiled a new play, interpreting the assassination story as an odd story of heroes. The play performed by Yucai School was based on the story. Almost at the same time, Nankai College in the north set up a student troupe and created and performed *New Village Head* (*Xin Cun Zheng*), *One Yuan* (*Yi Yuan Qian*) and other plays.

Dramas performed by students at schools extended beyond closed schools in the name of modern drama. In 1905, the students of Shanghai Minli High School began to stage performances outside the school. The students, edified by dramas at school, had preliminary experience of performance and strived to serve society and promote drama innovation by using their immature drama performances. Then Wang Zhongsheng (1880–1911) recruited some drama fans and rehearsed *Black Slaves' Appeal to Heaven* (*Hei Nu Yu Tian Lu*), adapted from the famous American novel *Uncle Tom's Cabin*, under the name of Chunyang Society. It became the first professional modern drama troupe in China.

A stage photo of modern opera *Bad Family*, performed by Xinmin Society in 1913.

Chunyang Society performed many new plays, such as *New Camellia* (*Xin Cha Hua*), adapted from *The Lady of the Camellias* by French writer Alexandre Dumas, and such plays as *A Flower in the Sea of Sins* (*Nie Hai Hua*), *Revealing Original Shape in Officialdom* (*Guan Chang Xian Xing Ji*), *Qiu Jin* and *Xu Xilin*. All were adapted from popular novels.

During the late Qing Dynasty, modern dramas were in emerging and already loved by a number of educated people longing for new learning. Troupes and drama societies that exclusively performed modern dramas emerged and vanished quickly. Shanghai's modern drama counterparts often went to surrounding cities such as Wuxi, Suzhou, Nanjing, Wuhu, and Changzhou, and even Wuhan, Beijing, and Tianjin to perform. Due to the influence of modern drama performances in Shanghai, various regions witnessed modern drama organizations and performances as well.

Modern dramas sprang up in various regions around the country and some opera fans who were early interested in modern dramas in their early years gradually found the channel for their art to communicate with Chinese society and people.

Zheng Zhengqiu (1888–1935) was an important organizer of

A stage photo of *Thunderstorm*.

Shanghai's modern drama composition and performance activities in the early period of the Republic of China. He began his contact with modern dramas during the late Qing Dynasty and early period of Republic of China and gradually became interested in modern dramas. He made outstanding contributions to the development of modern dramas. He compiled *Bad Family* (*E Jia Ting*) based on current affairs at that time for the Minming Society which then rehearsed and performed such plays as the *Empress Dowager* (*Xi Tai Hou*) and *Laugh in the Sleeve* (*San Xiao Yin Yuan*). The plays were very popular with Shanghai audiences.

The performances of these modern dramas broke the dominance of traditional operas, enabling people to witness the possibility of the development of such modern dramas in China. Encouraged by that, Zheng Zhengqiu ran Xinmin Society by himself, adapting then prevailing Peking Opera plays such as *The Hate* (*Hen Hai*), *The Tablet of Blood and Tears* (*Xue Lei Bei*), *Lotus Nunnery* (*Lian Hua An*) and *Case of Killing Son* (*Sha Zi Bao*) into modern plays.

The modern dramas gradually incorporated people's cultural

and recreational life both in topics and content, becoming an integral part of urban culture. Gradually, the performances were transferred from theaters to various pleasure grounds. The so-called crude stage play or modern drama were used and accepted by many people at the time.

The Chinese Drama Society, set up with the advocacy of Chen Dabei (1887–1944) in 1922, brought together 48 member organizations across the country, most of which were school drama societies in various places, including student drama societies at Beijing's Tsinghua University, Beijing Higher Normal College, and Beijing Women's Higher Normal College.

Chen studied in France in his early years, and served as a teacher at a mission school in Suzhou after returning to China. Known as the No.1 Tragic Female Role in early modern dramas, he instead advocated non-professional dramas.

A more important change started with Hong Shen (1894–1955), Xiong Foxi (1900–1965) and Yu Shangyuan (1897–1970) who returned after studying in Europe and played a critical role in the development of modern dramas in the 1920s and the development of special characteristics of stage plays. They were the first Chinese opera workers who received complete western drama education and had a real understanding of western dramas. With their efforts, the common artistic features of such western drama styles, practices, and theoretical foundations really took root in China.

In 1933, Tang Huaiqiu (1898–1954) set up the Travel Drama Troupe of China in Shanghai, marking new stage in the history of the development of stage play. The troupe was the first professional state play troupe that could sustain and develop by means of performance incomes. It lasted 14 years.

Low comedy was an unexpected product of the development of modern dramas and crude stage plays in Shanghai and its surrounding areas. The low comedy mainly borrowed the form of modern dramas and was performed in Shanghai dialect. It marked another direction for the development of modern drama in China.

Having nurtured stable audiences in Shanghai and its surrounding areas, it is still popular today.

Cao Yu.

After its establishment, the Travel Drama Troupe of China staged tour performances in various cities, including the most popular play *Thunderstorm* (*Lei Yu*) by famous Chinese playwright Cao Yu. The emergence of Cao Yu showed that there were not only audiences for stage plays but also great librettos.

Cao Yu (1910–1996) was a stage play fan during his school years. Influenced by Zhang Boling (1876–1951), president of Nankai College, and his younger brother Zhang Pengchun (1892–1957), Cao joined Nankai Modern Drama Troupe, played a heroine in the play *Nora* and was a co-writer of *New Village Head* along with Zhang Pengchun. The two cooperated to translate Moliere's famous play *Miser* and adapted it to a three-act play called *Craze for Money* (*Cai Kuang*), where he played the heroine.

Cao Yu's drama road, from its outset, was guided and directed by Zhang Pengchun, a scholar with in-depth understanding of European and US dramas. The topic and style of his initial script *Thunderstorm* was directly linked to the drama trends in the Europe and the US. Cao Yu completed *Thunderstorm* before his graduation from college in 1933. He had conceived this play for five years. This four-act stage play was published the following year and quickly triggered a strong response. It was not only his maiden work, but also the play that made him famous and a representative of his work. In 1936 and 1937, Cao Yu had his important plays *Sunrise* (*Ri Chu*) and *Wilderness* (*Yuan Ye*) published. Cao Yu accomplished his most important drama creation before he was 30. Meanwhile, he enabled the creation of Chinese stage play and elevated it to a fairly high threshold. Cao Yu's three masterpieces became the unsurpassable classics for stage play writers in the decades that followed.

From modern dramas and crude stage plays to popular stage plays and low comedy, Chinese operas had a mature new theatrical form-stage play, which makes Chinese operas more diversified as a whole. Throughout 100 years, artists engaged in stage play creation and performance made a wide range of adjustments and changes to performing forms and styles of western stage plays based on the habits and tastes of the Chinese audiences, enabling their assimilation into Chinese culture. They finally took root in China and became one of the most influential opera styles. Cao Yu even allowed stage play to embody enduring values in the field of Chinese literature and the literary status of the young stage play, just like Yuan *zaju* with over 800 years history and Ming and Qing *chuanqi* involving the emergence of numerous outstanding playwrights, it is recognized by the times and audiences.

With Ups and Downs: Extending Its Global Presence

New Stage

Chinese Opera faced lots of uncertainties brought on by the frequent and intensive contact between China and the outside world from the mid 19th to the 20th century. Inevitably, it underwent huge changes in form, site and the rules of performance as it became subject to the overwhelming impact of the global wave of modernization exemplified by industrialized metropolises.

During the Qing Dynasty, opera houses—generally called tea houses—began to spring up in cities and towns all over China. Along with the popularity of Peking Opera, teahouse-styled buildings originally found in Peking as well as conventional patterns of watching spread to the whole country, focusing the development of Chinese Opera towards a market-oriented goal. Although Peking Opera contributed to the spread of tea houses, it was not the only type of opera performed as local residents remained faithful to their local styles.

Shanghai Tianchan Stage built in 1925, for the performance of Peking Opera only. It used to have more than 3,400 seats. Many well-known actors of Peking Opera, such as Mei Lanfang, Xun Huisheng, Ma Lianliang, Gai Jiaotian and Yu Zhenfei, performed on the stage.

From the beginning of 20th century, with the emergence of new stages, the most beloved sites of opera performance in China changed as well. In 1908, the Shanghai New Stage was completed. It didn't take long for new theaters to model themselves after the New Stage and the style swept the country in a few years.

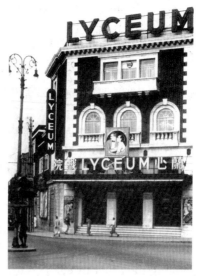

Shanghai Lyceum Theater, built in 1931. Mainly used for the performance of modern drama and concert.

In 1907, brothers Xia Yueshan (1868–1924) and Xia Yuerun (1878–1931)—owners of the Dangui Tea House—and Peking Opera artist Pan Yueqiao (1869–1928), along with a group of Chinese squires and merchants, launched and funded the costly project. Located alongside the Huangpu River, the Shanghai New Stage was completely different from traditional opera houses. It was the first Western style theater in China built for Chinese operas. Its architectural

An interior view of Lyceum Theater.

style was greatly influenced by Western theaters. The Xia brothers even went abroad to observe and study, visiting Japan and Europe.

The whole building of the New Stage was a large oval, with its spectator seats divided into three stories: the ground floor was called the hall, the second was for VIPs and the third for ordinary people. In this way, the capacity of the theater was greatly enlarged, and particularly the lines of vision of the audience could be improved: whether sitting in the main section or the upper circle, spectators would naturally face the stage; side tables which previously had been used for placing food and tea sets were taken away; the ground under the spectator seats was laid low in the front and high at the back, and the seats were set in rows on that sloping floor, which highlighted the only function of the New Stage—to enjoy the show. The style and patterns in Chinese traditional opera houses were thus entirely reversed.

The New Stage also set up an unprecedented semi-circular stage with both Chinese and western elements. With its front protruding a little bit, the stage actually faced the audience on three sides, which was actually a compromise between eastern and western designs because in tea houses, the stage of the traditional Chinese operas was designed as a square with only the back side draped, leaving the other three open to audience; while in normal Western theaters, two wings and the back side were all closed, only leaving the front for the audience.

For performers, different stage patterns required different performing techniques. In tea houses, performers had to take into account audiences sitting on three sides, i.e. 180° in their field of vision. In western theaters, they only had to focus on the front, which was the only direction in which the stage faced spectators. Therefore, though the New Stage adopted its architectural structure from the west, the design of the stage took into consideration the habits of Chinese audiences. Moreover, the new theater provided people with more convenient visual access to the stage by taking away two big poles commonly seen in front of the traditional tea houses stages.

The stage in the new theater was much bigger than in traditional tea houses, which meant performers could enjoy exponentially larger spaces to act and could use more backgrounds and props. Complex backdrops gradually became an important element of opera performances, thoroughly reversing the Chinese tradition. The birth of this western-style New Stage also helped induce the first generation of artistic stage designers in China. Zhang Yuguang

(1885–1968) was invited to become the stage director at the New Stage. He designed a great number of sceneries for the New Stage and other new theaters and is regarded as the originator of stage art in Chinese opera.

Just a few years after the founding of the New Stage, along with the sudden withering of old-fashioned tea houses, new-styled theaters spread wildly in Shanghai, which prompted the spread of Chinese Opera from Shanghai to other cities.

As competition in the performing market became increasingly fierce towards the end of 19th century, many new opera forms gradually emerged, the most representative of which was the "serialized drama" in Peking Opera.

After Peking Opera entered Shanghai and spread, serialized dramas provided a new way to attract a local audience. From the end of the 19th century to the beginning of the 20th, the Tianxian Tea House started to compose new serialized dramas with great response. The play *Miser* (*Tie Gong Ji*), for example, enjoyed tremendous success. The plots of *Miser* were based on historical facts. Jiangnan Prefect Xiang Rong and betrayed Taiping general Zhang Jiaxiang beset Nanjing with the Qing army and fight with the Taiping troops during the Taiping Heavenly Kingdom Period (also known as the Taiping Rebellion). *Miser* was written and performed by Wang Hongshou (1850–1925)—an actor in the Tianxian Tea House—with Zhao Songshou as the drummer. The story includes twelve single plays.

Miser embodied many symbolic elements of Shanghai Peking Opera. It was dynamic, lively and thrilling. The theme was simple. Rights and wrongs

Serialized drama

Serialized drama is a drama played in series. It usually presents a long story combined with a series of independent but interrelated plays. To maintain the interest of the audience, a certain amount of suspense is inserted into each play. A serialized drama often takes several days to finish. The first serialized dramas appeared in the royal palace during the Qing Dynasty. Different from the tradition of telling a new plot each day used in storytelling during the Tang and Song dynasties—in which performers spent successive days recounting long stories in words and songs—serialized dramas would only set up a new play after the previous one had concluded its round.

The stage appearance of Xue Juexian in *Bai Jinlong.*

in the story were perfect clear. Colorful lighting was substantially employed on the stage. Actors and actresses performed not only with real swords and spears, but also used stunts like jumping through a ring of fire and playing with guns or imitating western military training, ushering a new stage of acrobatic fighting with real weapons in Chinese opera. *Miser* later became the most representative and beloved play among Peking Opera in Shanghai.

From the prevailing of Kunqu to the more action-based derivations of Peking Opera, artistic techniques in singing, reading, acting and fighting became more important but, as a result, plot lines were neglected. The flourishing of local dramas all over the country and serialized dramas in Shanghai helped save Chinese Opera from a distorted development route.

During the period of Republic of China, operas were mainly performed in cities and easily yielded to the impact of the emerging mechanism of commercialization. At that time, the changes of Cantonese Opera attracted the most attention. Cantonese Opera was also regarded as the most typical specimen in the wave of drama commercialization.

Going through the recovery at the late of Qing Dynasty, Cantonese Opera entered its golden age during the Republic of China. The emergence of new style theaters led to the explosion of new plays in Cantonese Opera, which were mainly appreciated by ordinary urban residents, whose interest and tastes also boosted the evolution of the Opera.

In Cantonese Opera, both singing and fighting were cherished and performers tended to dress in more dazzling and odd clothes. Yet the greatest change was found in the plays to be performed. Just between the 1920s to the 1930s, thousands of new plays were

Being Conferred Prime Minister by Six Kingdoms, the most famous serial Cantonese Opera. It has extensive scenes and rich characters.

written just as the subject of Cantonese Opera changed.

Although it used to be similar to that in Han Opera and Peking Opera, the subject of Cantonese Opera had a bias towards family ethics and love stories. For example, the play *Bai Jinlong*, adapted from an American movie, talked about the love story between Bai Jinlong and Zhang Yuniang. Bai Jinlong was the son of a rich man. To court Zhang Yuniang—a girl came from a declining noble family—he pretends to be a servant in Zhang's house and redeems Zhang's valuable jewelry to win the favor of the girl. After she is seized by two street lechers, Bai disguises as a western woman and rescues Zhang. In the end, the couple gets married. The play's fabulous elements, compact layout and famous actor—Xue Juexian (1904–1956)—contributed to its nine-month continuous run and set a new record in Cantonese Opera history. As love stories became common in theaters, *dan* (the female role) gradually rose to be equally important as *sheng* (the male role).

The changes in Cantonese Opera during the period of the Republic of China were obviously related to commercialization. Urban theaters and company operations made profits a more decisive factor in the changes to the internal mechanisms of Cantonese Opera.

In the late Qing Dynasty when the most luxurious opera system in Chinese history emerged in rural areas around Guangdong and Guangxi Provinces, about 158 persons were needed to form a troupe, which would perform in a period of five days. They usually started a show in the afternoon and would not conclude until nine or ten the next morning. Each time a troupe went to a new place, it generated great excitement and created a bustling atmosphere.

Tremendous organization, huge cost and strict performing regulations won support from rich elites. However, it was against the rules to operate in urban theaters. Therefore, after the political and social structure that propped up the original troupe mechanism collapsed alongside the traditional social structure, commercial benefit became the most direct and effective impulse to the changes in the performance system. The historic turn in the development direction in Cantonese Opera also helped bring many well-known evolve.

One important example was the 10-year competition between the Jue Xiansheng Troupe led by Xue Juexian and the Taiping Troupe led by Ma Shizeng (1900–1964). This decade-long rivalry was regarded as the core driving force of Cantonese Opera towards the mid and late period of the Republic of China. The rivalry also greatly inspired performers, playwrights and directors in Guangzhou and Hong Kong. As a result, Cantonese Opera became predominant in Southeast Asia and spread globally as people from Lingnan traveled abroad.

Throughout the 1920s and 1930s, various musical instruments, including western ones, started appearing in Cantonese Opera, leading to tremendous changes in the music used. Back to the late Qing Dynasty, the main musical instruments used in Cantonese Opera were the *erxian* (a two-string fiddle) and the *yueqin* (a plucked lute with a wooden body, a short fretted neck, and four strings tuned in pairs), or the gong, drum and cymbal. During the Republic of China Period, the *erhu* (Chinese two-string violin) became the most popular instrument, replacing the two-string fiddle. At the same time, the *qinqin* (a plucked lute with a wooden body and fretted neck) took the place of *yueqin*. Western musical instruments that were frequently used were violin and saxophone; guitar, jazz drum and electric guitar sometimes showed up. Music in Cantonese Opera thus experienced fundamental changes during that time.

All these changes in Cantonese Opera during the first half of the 20th century were, to a large extent, influenced by western popular art and American movies. It was not until the 1950s that Cantonese Opera sought to return to tradition and the charm of the national play.

Mei Lanfang—Going to the World

The status and influence of Peking Opera made rapid strides during the period of the Republic of China. After Tan Xinpei passed away, people gradually reached a consensus on the new three of the most distinguished people in Peking Opera: Yu Shuyan (1890–1943), Yang Xiaolou (1877–1938) and Mei Lanfang (1894–1961).

Yu Shuyan was greatly self-disciplined in digging into Tan Xinpei's artistic performance despite of the social unrest during the early stages of the Republic of China. By attending each of Tan's live show, Yu learnt by heart Tan's tunes, words, gestures and the overall performing process, and made rapid progress. After Tan Xinpei passed away, Yu Shuyan not only did not give up his learning, but tried all the possible indirect approaches to learn from Tan. Concentrating on his studies for over ten years, Yu finally managed to propel Tan's art to a new high: the essence was kept, and the previous blemish in Tan's singing almost eliminated.

Yu was just like the mainstay to pure art in the wave of commercialization. He was very strict in his art. Plays he polished were all regarded as perfection. Yu's greatest contribution was passing on perfect Peking Opera performances—that was why he was recognized as a master.

Yu Shuyan plays the role of Huang Zhong in *The Battle of Dingjunshan*, which is a classic representative of Tan Xinpei's performance. But Yu not only gained the essence of Tan, but also brought in new ideas.

Mei Lanfang was the most influential master in the world during the period of the Republic of China. Born to a family of Peking Opera performers in Beijing, he got his first public show at Guanghe Theater at the age of 10. The play was *Fairy Couple* (*Tian Xian Pei*). After that, Mei Lanfang's fame gradually grew. He gave his first performance in Shanghai in 1913, which soon dominated the vast area south of the Yangtze River. One year later, he went to Shanghai again and performed several famous traditional plays including *Drunk Concubine* (*Gui Fei Zui Jiu*) for 34 successive days. By studying from different role categories in Peking Operas including *qingyi*, *huadan* and *daomadan*, Mei Lanfang finally developed his own unique style in singing, ways of speaking, music and dressing. His singing, in particular, won him a tremendous reputation and contributed to the birth of the "School of Mei." In 1927 in the Chinese first evaluated famous *dan* performers—a contest done by the *Shuntian Times*—Mei Lanfang, known for his solid foundation in artistic knowledge, beautiful voice and makeup, was elected as one of the Four Famous *Dan* Actors along with Cheng Yanqiu (1904–1958), Shang Xiaoyun (1900–1976) and Xun Huisheng (1900–1968).

Mei Lanfang was an idol of the time. His characters integrated people's aesthetic desire for classical beauty in women and brought

A group photo of the "Four Famous *Dan* Actors" in 1949. From left to right: Xun Huisheng, Mei Lanfang, Shang Xiaoyun and Cheng Yanqiu.

Male *Dan*
Male *dan* refers to the male actors who perform female roles in Chinese traditional theater. It was commonly seen in Peking Opera and other kinds of operas during the Qing Dynasty. Plays in love stories usually had some intimate scenes but the Qing governments strictly prohibited female performers from acting with male actors, because it was regarded as a violation of social morals and ethics. Therefore, with women excluded from private troupes in the homes of Qing officials, men played every character in a drama. That is how male *dan* came into being. Female performers existed, too, but they had to form an independent troupe where all the members were women. The prohibitions were gradually eliminated after 1921. By strict and systematic training, a good male *dan* could skillfully use his physiological features to better present the attitude, gestures and elegant beauty of the female figures in plays.

the *dan* to a new and historic high. But Mei Lanfang's more significant contributions were his successive visits to Japan, the US and the Soviet Union, presenting the charm of Chinese traditional operas to the world.

In December 1929, Mei Lanfang and his troupe traveled to the US to perform. On February 16th, 1930, he officially launched his show at the 49th Street Theater in Broadway of New York. Thinking that the American audience had little knowledge about Chinese traditional operas, Mei made a series of preparations before he came. He tried to know the interest of American spectators and printed beautiful advertising materials as well as books on Chinese Opera, which contained detailed pictures and illustrations. After he arrived, Mei Lanfang asked Zhang Pengchun to be the host, who was an expert on dramas and had experience studying in the America. Play lists and performing patterns were also

A stage photo from *Farewell My Concubine* played by Mei Lanfang and Yang Xiaolou in 1922. Yang enjoyed the title of "Master of *wusheng* (a male martial role)" in Peking Opera. The cooperation between the two is superb and is regarded as an immortal classic.

During his visit to the US, Mei Lanfang meets with Charlie Chaplin, the comedy master.

adjusted to fit the habits of the new audience. Before each show, Zhang Pengchun would give the audience a simple introduction in English, enhancing communication with American spectators. During the six-month visit in the US, Mei Lanfang acted in many cities, such as New York, Chicago, San Francisco, Los Angeles and Honolulu, with tremendous success.

Though the origin of Chinese Opera in the US can be traced back to the earliest Chinese workers in America, the real start of Chinese traditional operas entering into mainstream American society was Mei Lanfang's visit. Mei's artistic performance caught the attention of most influential opera scholars, critics and

During his visit to the US, Mei Lanfang meets with the Governor of Honolulu.

mainstream media. Mei Lanfang was also awarded an honorary doctorate by Pomona College and the University of Southern California.

Invited by the International Culture Exchange Association of the Soviet Union, Mei Lanfang visited the country to perform with his troupe in 1935. The delegation invited as advisers Zhang Pengchun and Yu Shangyuan, opera scholars with solid understanding of both oriental and occidental style; while the USSR organized a specialized committee led by Director Stanislavski to welcome the Chinese guests. The members included Danchenko, Meyerhold, Eisenstein and other world-class luminaries. Mei Lanfang put on a number of performances in Moscow and Leningrad, to which large audiences that included performers and students thronged.

The performances deeply impressed foreign opera artists. Meyerhold, a famous director, even commented exaggeratedly: "After seeing how Mei Lanfang uses his hand in plays, the only thing Russian performers could do is to cut their own hands off." Before Mei left Moscow, a round-table conference was held by the USSR International Culture Exchange Association. Mei

Mei Lanfang visits the Soviet Union in 1935.

Lanfang, Zhang Pengchun, Yu shangyuan attended along with Stanislavski, Danchenko, Meyerhold and Eisenstein, as well as famous musicians and dancers from the Soviet Union. They all spoke extremely highly of Mei. Bertolt Brecht, a famous German director who happened to be in the USSR watched Mei Lanfang's performance and was deeply moved. In his article *Alienation Effects in Chinese Acting* he proposed new opera theories and set up a unique system of opera performance by discussing Mei Lanfang's performance in plays like *The Fisherman's Revenge (Da Yu Sha Jia)*.

Concluding his performance in the Soviet Union, Mei Lanfang continued his shows in Europe and studied foreign plays. His visit to the Soviet Union was much more culturally significant than that of any other Chinese opera performer because this time in Moscow, the deep discussion and communication between Mei Lanfang and well-known opera performers from the USSR and east Europe was recognized as the first face-to-face dialogue that reflected each party's ideas on operas. Thanks to the dialogue, Chinese Opera started opening to the world.

Years later, especially after the 1950s, Chinese Opera showed its unique charm time and time again. After the 1980s, such exchanges

Mei Lanfang receives French guests in his house in Beijing.

become more frequent and intensive. The footprints of Chinese Opera can now be found all over Europe and western operas have much more opportunities to come into China. In the last hundred years, western operas from classic to post-modernist have all been introduced to China, to some extent, influencing modern Chinese dramatists.

Improvement to the Traditional Opera and "Model Opera"

On October 1st, 1949, the People's Republic of China was founded. Changes in the social system also resulted in significant changes to its plays. The new government valued traditional operas highly and asked the Ministry of Culture to set up a specialized bureau on drama improvement. Relevant departments were also set up in local governments and cadres were sent alongside troupes to enhance "opera improvements," which were composed of three parts: Improving the people, the mechanism and the operas.

In September 1949, four artists of traditional opera were invited to the first plenary session of the Chinese People's Political Consultative Conference. They were Mei Lanfang, Zhou Xinfang

(1895–1975), Cheng Yanqiu and Yuan Xuefen. In 1954 during the first National People's Congress, seven opera performers were elected as deputies to the NPC, including Peking Opera artists Mei Lanfang, Zhou Xinfang and Cheng Yanqiu, Shaoxing Opera artist Yuan Xuefen, Yu Opera artist Chang Xiangyu (1923–2004), Chuan Opera artist Chen Shufang (1924–1996) and Lüju Opera artist Lang Xianfen. As a result, they could directly participate in national political affairs, reflecting a dramatic enhancement of the social status of opera performers. In local regions, there were also a large number of opera artists that became deputies and committee members of the local NPC and CPPCC.

For thousands of years, drama actors in China had been considered as "ragtag." Even after the Yuan Dynasty, when opera scripts became more accepted as literary styles by the mainstream due to the achievements of Yuan Drama and Ming-Qing Fiction, opera performances were still subject to all kinds of discrimination. Only after the founding of the new China in 1949, did those actors and actresses finally manage to climb from low position and received the political honor, revealing the new government' s recognition of their value and the social status they deserved.

In the meantime, the improvement on the ownership of opera troupes was gradually launched. The majority of the previous

A group photo of some representatives from literary and art circles during the First Session of the National People's Congress of China in 1954, including opera performers Yuan Xuefen, Cheng Yanqiu, Chang Xiangyu, Zhou Xinfang and Mei Lanfang.

A group photo of performers taking part in the First National Chinese Opera Festival in 1952.

troupes were privately owned. Their ownership changed and they became "Republic Troupes" where all the actors and actresses shared joint ownership at first and eventually became national troupes guided or directly affiliated to and managed by the governments. The improvement of the mechanism in cities also involved theaters and the existing performing systems. Since the Song Dynasty, opera performances have become more commercialized. The improvements went a long way towards strengthening publicity and educational functions and putting less emphasis on profit, which would play a less significant role over time. As a result, the original theater business model was basically abolished. The improvements also included a series of measures named "stage purification," such as dismissing prop managers, not allowing performers to during while acting and officially removing tea and candy shops from theaters.

These measures changed habit that had been formed during the late Qing Dynasty, when opera was played in tea houses, resulting in the disappearance of many distinctive customs from traditional theaters. The ultimate goal was to highlight the completeness and artistic purity of stage shows.

The core of the opera improvement campaign lied in the reform of the plays, i.e. improving a large number of traditional plays. Guided by cadres assigned by the government, dozens of plays were defined as models in the "improvement" and were performed during the First National Chinese Opera Festival held by the Ministry of Culture in 1952. Attended by over 1,600 performers from 37 troupes of 23 opera categories covering most of the provinces, it was considered the first national opera show in Chinese history. During the big show, 87 plays were performed, including 63 traditional ones, 11 new historical plays and 8 modern ones.

The attitudes and measures towards the traditional plays by authorities could be clearly revealed in the national opera festival, during which the most noteworthy plays were three versions of

A stage photo of Shaoxing Opera *Butterfly Lovers*.

Butterfly Lovers (Liang Shan Bo Yu Zhu Ying Tai) — the Shaoxing Opera version, the Peking Opera version and the Chuan Opera version — and two versions of *Tale of the White Snake (Bai She Zhuan)*, the Peking Opera and Shaoxing Opera versions.

The Shaoxing Opera version of *Butterfly Lovers* was based on *Sad Story of Liang and Zhu (Liang Zhu Ai Shi)* performed by Yuan Xuefen. Being regarded as a model in the "improvement," it had been highly thought of by the government even before the national opera festival. *Butterfly Lovers* originated from a widespread folk tale. It tells of a romantic but sad love story: Zhu Yingtai, the heroine, is the only child of a rich family in Shangyu of Zhejiang. She loves reading, but can only pursue her studies disguised as a man because women did not have the right to receive education at the time. On her way to Hangzhou in search of a better education, she meets Liang Shanbo who has the same plan. Having the same temperament, the two become sworn brothers and forge a deep friendship during three years of study. When the study period is over, Zhu returns home and Liang insists on seeing Zhu off. Distressed at the coming departure, Zhu frequently implies to Liang in various metaphors that she is a woman and that she is determined to be with him for all eternity, but unfortunately Liang is a bookworm and does not get the message. Months later, he finally discovers Zhu is a woman and happily goes to Zhu's family

Shaoxing Opera *Butterfly Lovers*, performed by Zhejiang Xiaobaihua Shaoxing Opera Troupe. The role of Liang Shanbo is played by Mao Weitao.

to propose, but her father has already arranged for her to marry Ma Wencai, the son of a local official.

Liang and Zhu meet in a pavilion in Zhu's house, but can only cry at the ironic circumstances set by fate. Liang is desperate and heartbroken. His health gradually deteriorates until he becomes seriously ill and dies. Zhu Yingtai falls into great despair and sadness after hearing the news. On her wedding day, she insists to take a compass during the procession, which allows her to visit Liang's grave first. When she approaches the grave, mysterious whirlwinds and thunders suddenly break out and the tomb opens. Zhu throws herself into the grave to join Liang Shanbo. At exactly that moment, two beautiful butterflies emerge from the grave, dancing together. It is said to be the spirits of the couple cannot be separated ever after death. Over the decades, different versions of similar stories have emerged.

The Shaoxing Opera version of *Butterflies Lovers* is best known in China. Classic parts in the play, such as *18 Mile Farewell*, describing how Liang Shanbo sees Zhu Yingtai off, and *Meeting in the Pavilion*, when Liang is shocked when he goes to propose, are the most enjoyed by people.

The Opera is a representative production in the campaign of "opera improvement." It was made into a color movie and received supreme marks in Europe, especially in Eastern European countries. This great opera classic, enriched by numerous performers over thousands of years and repeatedly polished by multiple authors, has gradually moved towards perfection. It has been endowed with even more cultural significance after careful adaptations in the 1950s.

Similar cases can be found all over the country. Most traditional plays could not be performed during the "opera improvement" since they did not fit the requirements of ideology. Still, the "improvement" had a positive impact by making the plays more delicate through the details.

The artistic career of Mei Lanfang also demonstrates from another prospective the huge impact of the "opera improvement."

Following the tremendous success of his visit to the US and the Soviet Union, Mei Lanfang started to underscore the classical features of his play and tried his best to polish his representative plays with the knowledge he acquired from Kunqu Opera, which is known for its delicateness.

The eight most prestigious of these plays are also called the "Eight Mei's Plays." These plays gradually emerged and included *Drunk Concubine* (*Gui Fei Zui Jiu*), *Farewell My Concubine* (*Ba Wang Bie Ji*), *Surprising Double Meeting* (*Qi Shuang Hui*), *The Returning Love* (*Feng Huan Chao*), *The Cosmos Sword* (*Yu Zhou Feng*), *Hate between Life and Death* (*Sheng Si Hen*), *Goddess of Luo River* (*Luo Shen*) and *Interrupted Dream in Peony Pavilion* (*You Yuan Jing Meng*). After the 1950s, Mei Lanfang insisted on acting in those plays, while allowed his performance skills to reach a new high.

In 1959 Mei Lanfang wrote and acted in the new play *Mu Guiying Taking Command* (*Mu Gui Ying Gua Shuai*), which is a representative work of his late years and the first new play he had

Mei Lanfang plays the role of Mu Guiying in *Mu Guiying Taking Command*.
Mei is senior-aged but vigorous and energetic.

written since entering middle age. The play was adapted from an opera with the same title performed by Ma Jinfeng, a well-known Yuju Opera actress.

The play was based on the most fantastic part of *Generals of the Yang Clan* (*Yang Jia Jiang*), an extremely popular story in China. Though only a very few words can be found in historical records about General Yang Jiye fighting with Jin troops during the Northern Song Dynasty, those records branched into a story with huge structure and numerous figures and plots, many chapters of which have been adapted into classic plays of Peking Opera and other opera categories.

Tan Xinpei earned his prestige from playing *The Tragedy at the Li*

Mei Lanfang plays the role of Concubine Yang in *Drunk Concubine*. He is
in his senior then, yet his performance is still appealing and intoxicating.

Ling Monument (Tuo Zhao Peng Bei) and *Hongyang Grave (Hong Yang Dong)*, which are part of the story in *Generals of the Yang Clan*. Also excerpted from the story, *The fourth Son of the Yang Family Visits His Mother (Si Lang Tan Mu)* can be regarded as one of the most dynamic and vigorous plays since the birth of Peking Opera. Being one of the important roles in the story, the legendary figure of Mu Guiying has been completely created by folk artists.

Her experience, especially as she takes command to fight the enemy troops in her late years, is described to the greatest extent. Several generations of the Yang family sacrifice their lives for the country, leaving only womenfolk. But when the enemies invade again and no other generals can be dispatched, the Yang family becomes the only hope for the court and the country. The version *Mu Guiying Taking Command* designed and performed by Mei Lanfang is based on this story. Facing the invasion by the Western Xia Dynasty, the emperor has no choice but to ask the elderly female general Mu Guiying to fight for the country. Mu Guiying intends to refuse, because on one hand the court used to be extremely mean and indifferent to the Yang family; on the other, it reminds her of a sad truth that except Yang Wenguang, the only live son, other family members are all widows because their husbands have laid down their lives for the country. But thinking of the present national crisis and persuaded by her grandmother-in-law, she finally determines to take command.

Mei Lanfang was in his sixties in 1959, and that was his first time acting as an old woman. To nobody's surprise, he performed extremely well, especially when the seal of commander was held, the figure he played soon transformed from a retired housewife into an honorable general. In the session of *Receiving the Seal*, Mu Guiying sang as follows:

Suddenly the sound of drums thunders in my ears, evoking my previous aspirations. I was so brave and awe-inspiring in the past, leading my people in the front line, with innumerable enemies beheaded under my horse. I will fulfill my duties as long as I am alive; how can I just watch the enemies seizing our towns! The king of the enemy is not worth bothering; my sword could kill millions of his men. If I don't take the command, who else will? If I don't lead the troops, who else will? Quickly get me armed; I will bring my seal, take command and rally the troops!

Mei Lanfang concluded his artistic career with *Mu Guiying Taking Command*. Through his work, he notes that Chinese Opera, after more than eight hunderd years of development, can still pursue art and self-perfection even in a society that is undergoing tremendous changes.

Since the 1950s, how to express modern subjects in the form of traditional operas had been a big concern for government and artists.

It was not difficult for the newly born modern play to present modern subjects. The cooperation between playwright Lao She (1899–1966) and director Jiao Juyin (1905–1975) in the founding process of Beijing People's Art Theater (BPAT) created a new national style for the BPAT and also for Chinese modern plays.

While directing Lao She's works *Dragon Beard Ditch* (*Long Xu Gou*) and *Teahouse* (*Cha Guan*) in particular, Jiao Juyin, who adored the system of performance set up by Stanislavski, a famous director in the Soviet Union, tried to make the BPAT a base to put Stanislavski' s theories into practice. He required actors and actresses to form a "mind image" of the characters they would play to "experience" the roles. Jiao Juyin was the first modern Chinese director to create his own style. Under his guidance, the BPAT managed to make progress and gradually approached maturity.

A stage photo from the initial performance of *Teahouse* in 1958.

Teahouse has been an evergreen play for decades. The picture is a stage photo of *Teahouse* performed by Beijing People's Art Theatre in recent years.

Teahouse is an immortal masterpiece. Just in the first scene, the playwright arranged dozens of lively figures in as short a period of time as ten minutes. The work has extremely vivid languages and a unique structure, which was designed based on the author's deep investigation of society and history. As a play with a high degree of "prose trend," it abandons the traditional principles told in textbooks but "shows" the changes of a teahouse in Beijing in three different ages, with no conflict and no story line. It is not a history either, for it only includes several parts of the story. In those parts, Lao She managed to make the figures live on stage by employing a unique sense of humor that is extremely expressive and embodies Beijing's characteristics.

But traditional dramatists in the 1950s were bothered with great puzzles, for it seemed rather difficult to make the new opera preserve its artistic value while achieving the goals of propaganda and education. After 1964, as public performances of many traditional operas started to be restricted, writing modern operas turned out to be the only choice for dramatists.

"Model Opera" was the most important production in the field of Chinese Opera in the 1960s. It came into being as a traditional opera integrated into modern society.

In 1964, a national show of modern Peking Opera was held in Beijing, where 29 troupes from institutions directly under the Ministry of Culture, Beijing and Shanghai performed 35 plays. It was another tremendous party of opera held by the country after the National Chinese Opera Festival. Later, local governments began to organize their own joint performances of modern plays. In 1965, another round of modern play performances, basically Peking Opera, was held throughout the country. To a large extent, opera was politicized, which resulted in its unprecedented position in society.

The stories of the "Model Opera" are usually integrated with both strong political intentions and great legendary narration, which could be best illustrated by *Taking Tiger Mountain by Strategy* (*Zhi Qu Wei Hu Shan*). *Taking Tiger Mountain by Strategy* is a "Model Opera" that appeared and was shaped earlier than others. The story is based on the novel *Tracks in the Snowy Forest* (*Lin Hai Xue Yuan*), which in turn is based on real incidents in northeast China during the Chinese Civil War. The story takes place most of the time in a stronghold of bandits. Yang Zirong, the hero, disguised himself as a bandit and acted as an inside man for the government. War and espionage, danger and suspense make this play extremely dramatic. It was later adopted into many versions for the stage. The version by the Shanghai Troupe of Peking Opera *Taking Tiger Mountain by Strategy* won the highest praise and was popularized as a model, according to which troupes all over China performed this play.

Characterization of figures was the priority for dramatists while adapting "Model Opera" for the stage, because audiences would only be politically educated when the figures' political character won their applause and respect. But due to long modifying and polishing, those "Model Opera" reached an extremely high level of plots development, language, especially in performance and music.

The Legend of the Red Lantern (*Hong Deng Ji*), jointly adapted by Weng Ouhong (1909–1994), one of the best playwrights of Peking Opera, and A Jia (1907–1994), one of the best directors, could be regarded as the one that has made the highest artistic achievements among all the "Model Opera."

In the scene of *Telling the Revolutionary History of the Family*, the integrated spoken and singing of Grandma Li is most appealing. Weng Ouhong learnt the form from similar scenes in traditional operas like *Story-Telling with Severed Arm* (*Duan Bi Shuo Shu*) and *Orphan of Zhao*. But since the atmosphere is more intense in *The Legend of the Red Lantern*, the same method works better.

Another typical scene is *Attending the Banquet to Debate with Jiu Shan*, where a fierce battle of words manages to attract all of people' attention. The new play has more intense arrangement in storylines and shaper conflicts between figures than in traditional ones such as *The Heroes' Feast* (*Qun Ying Hui*), and the actors and actresses performing were so recognized by the audience that whenever the play was mentioned at that time, people would talk of their names and the roles they played: Li Shaochun's Li Yuhe, Liu Changyu's Li Tiemei, Gao Yuqian's Grandma Li and Yuan Shihai's Jiu Shan.

"Model Opera" usually offer a clear distinction between right and wrong. In such plays, characters are divided into two categories, either good or bad, which can be recognized by their different performances.

Model Opera
Since the 1960s a group of well-designed opera plays emerged whose subjects and ways of presenting were recognized by the authorities. Revised several times, those plays finally became the model for troupes of different opera categories all over the country. In May 1967, eight plays were officially named as "Model Opera." They were *Taking Tiger Mountain by Strategy* (*Zhi Qu Wei Hu Shan*), *The Legend of the Red Lantern* (*Hong Deng Ji*), *Raid on the White Tiger Regiment* (*Qi Xi Bai Hu Tuan*) and *The Harbor* (*Hai Gang*) of Peking Opera, *The Red Detachment of Women* (*Hong Se Niang Zi Jun*) and *The White-Haired Girl* (*Bai Mao Nü*), as well as *Shachipang* (*Sha Jia Bang*) of symphony. The eight "Model Opera" were showed during a show in Beijing that lasted 37 days and included 218 performances. For a long period of time, those model plays were the only ones allowed by the authorities and greatly impressed hundreds of millions of Chinese people.

A stage photo of Model Opera *Taking Tiger Mountain by Strategy*.

For example, positive characters will generally strike some poses on stage. Action designs in other plays are also praiseworthy. In the scene of *Beating Tiger and Going up the Mountain in Taking Tiger Mountain by Strategy*, a series of actions of Yang Zirong have really distinctive patterns, regardless of the motions or structures. *Raid on the White Tiger Regiment*, after absorbing and adapting the patterns from traditional Peking Operas, manages to create extremely elegant actions of its own.

In the scene of *Mental Battle in Shachipang (Sha Jia Bang)*, the antiphonal singing among A Qingsao, Hu Chuankui and Diao Deyi is regarded as a classic in the field of musical design. The three figures, standing on stage together, not only have solos that express their respective mental activities, but also sing through antiphonal dialogues that show their interaction and conflict.

Loose and tight emotions and vivid sentence patterns make the scene an example in "Model Opera," the most popular part in *Shachipang* and also the most stunning section among all the "Model

Model Opera *The Legend of the Red Lantern*. Grandma Li tells Li Tiemei about the family's revolutionary history.

Opera." It highlights the achievements "Model Opera" make in adapting music. To better present subtle and complicated relations and disclose their respective characters, the three figures employ the roles of *dan*, *sheng* and *jing* of Peking Opera that are totally different from but also complementary to each other. Especially the clashing antiphonal singing between A Qingsao and Diao Deyi successfully pushes the figures' emotion to a climax. It is a model of both musicalized drama and dramatized music. The musical achievements in *Taking Tiger Mountain by Strategy* are also well recognized. The music adopted in *Beating Tiger and Going up the Mountain* is the most brilliant part in the play's accompaniment. The beautiful melody is greatly cherished even today for it evokes old memories of that time. Later, the introduction of symphony in *Azalea Mountain* (*Du Juan Shan*) also greatly enriches the musical pattern that can be employed in Peking Opera.

"Model Opera" didn't break away completely with the musical styles of traditional Peking Opera. Actually, since the music had

A stage photo of Model Opera *Shachipang*.

to be in accordance with the characters and emotions of the heroic figures, to be identical with the rhythm and spirits at that time, it brought something of a renewal and update of the traditional music. That's also why "Model Opera" are still appealing today.

During the Cultural Revolution (1966–1976) when "Model Opera" monopolized Chinese opera stages, a great number of outstanding opera performers all over China were persecuted and playwriting was also affected by politics. However, playwrights of different opera categories in different places stuck with their art; even if they were ordered to write or perform plays with purely political purposes. They would try to make the plays as perfect as possible, which from another prospective manifests the efforts of those artists in presenting modern subjects with traditional forms.

Forward-looking Chinese Theater

At the end of the 1970s, another tremendous change took place. The reform and opening-up allowed China carefully review its opera tradition and calmly face the world. After finally breaking away from political fetters, plenty of traditional plays resurfaced. Films including Shaoxing Opera *Dream of the Red Chamber* (*Hong Lou Meng*) and Huangmei Opera *Fairy Couple* (*Tian Xian Pei*) soon attracted large audiences back into theaters. Artists enjoyed more freedom. Many dramatists transformed their reflection of real life into artistic creation, bringing Chinese Opera to its most prosperous stage since the 1950s.

The new epoch gave dramatists more access to the world and resulted in a swarm of new ideas and notions. The exploration in the forms of plays marked the gradual revitalization of Chinese Opera. Since the 1980s, a group of playwrights and directors dedicated to Exploration Plays learnt from and imitated modern plays from the west, creating new theater atmosphere. Many of them, represented by Lin Zhaohua, became pioneers in modern play exploration.

The western school of modernism opened a window for them, helping them find efficient instruments to break the handcuffs

Built in 1954, the Capital Theatre is the first professional theatre for modern plays in Beijing. Even today, to many modern play fans, it is still their "sacred place."

of political dogmas that had dominated the Chinese Opera for decades and strongly restricted art development. The play *Absolute Signal* (*Jue Dui Xin Hao*) directed by Lin Zhaohua was the first important Exploration Plays, and is recognized as the origin of a little theater play campaign in modern Chinese society.

Absolute Signal was shown in the upstairs dining hall of the Beijing Peoples' Art Theater in November, 1982. It made some breakthroughs compared with the play script.

The action happens in the back of a van driving at night. As escorts, Xiaohao and his master are on duty. Later, they meet Heizi and Mifeng who asks to take a ride. Xiaohao and his old friend Heizi both adore Mifeng, creating a triangle relationship. Heizi, who intends to rob the goods in the van along with his fellow bandits, the master, who is always on the alert, and careless Xiaohao shape into another triangle relationship. It is easy to guess

Absolute Signal, a little theatre play directed by Lin Zhaohua.

the ending: The conspiracy is crashed and two good youths find hope in their love.

The script arranges the whole story in the carriage of a moving van. The carriage is closed and static, which is symbolic but also challenging. Strongly supported by Cao Yu, Director of Beijing People's Art Theater, *Absolute Signal* was an extraordinary success. The play has immature elements that cannot be avoided in epoch alternation. When showed in a dining hall, not typical place for a performance, it reveals its intentional rebellion from the USSR's big theater artistic style that had been carefully followed since the 1950s.

The Bus Stop (*Che Zhan*), another play by Director Lin Zhaohua, has profound meaning.

The story happens in a bus stop in a suburb of a city on a Saturday evening. Many people intend to take the bus to go downtown. They wait for the bus anxiously, but the bus never shows up. Complaining and worried, people wait in vain. The time flies until they have all stood here for ten years and are old,

A scene of *The Bus Stop*, which is also a little theatre play.

To live or to Die, a modern opera of Lin Zhaohua in 2007.

humpbacked and grey-haired. Only then, people find the stop board has been blurred for quite a long time and remember a silent man, who used to stay here and wait for the bus, but left quietly and walked to the destination.

Obviously, *The Bus Stop* is an imitation of Samuel Beckett's *Waiting for Godot*. Becket is a western absurdist master who mixes criticism of the real world. The play thus not only reflects China's reality at that time, but is also a version of *Waiting for Godot* written in Chinese. The short play struggles with metaphysical meaning. At least, through the depiction of a group of people waiting for the bus inflexibly, it explores people's confusion—a common theme at that time.

The Bus Stop generated exciting responses. If we say *Absolute Signal* exemplifies the beginning of Chinese modern plays and their breaking away from Ibsenism and the system of Stanislavski, then *The Bus Stop* is the result of that breakaway.

Chinese little theater plays originated from *Absolute Signal* and *The Bus Stop* developed into a brilliant sight in Chinese Opera in the next twenty years.

Peking Opera, *Cao Cao and Yang Xiu*. Cao Cao is acted by Shang Changrong, and Yang Xiu is performed by Yan Xingpeng.

The development of traditional operas also contributed to the achievements in opera at that time. *Cao Cao and Yang Xiu*, created and performed by the Shanghai Troupe of Peking Opera, is the most classic work among all the new plays during that time. In a joint performance of new Peking Opera plays held by the Ministry of Culture in Tianjin in December 1988, *Cao Cao and Yang Xiu* won top spot as Excellent New Play of Peking Opera. Later, at China's First Peking Opera Festival, it again received the only gold prize.

Actually, it is not so easy to find the style and trends of the 1980s in the dramatic creation *Cao Cao and Yang Xiu*. The play doesn't appear appropriate for those times of exploration and innovation. But just because of its inopportuneness, the playwright, director and main actors could take the time to carefully polish the work. The two leading actors, Shang Changrong and Yan Xingpeng, are extraordinary artists who thoroughly convey the charm of traditional Peking Opera.

The structure of the play is totally different from traditional Peking Opera. There are many plays of Peking Opera whose hero is Cao Cao and they all have a relatively complete story line. *Cao*

Fairy Couple, a classic play of Huangmei Opera, in which a number of wonderful sections have enjoyed great popularity.

Cao and Yang Xiu is outlined by the rivalry of the two figures, the clashes in their characters and the ups and downs in their fates. That structure is quite similar to the idea adopted in Chinese painting but turns out to be more valuable in plays for its novelty and uniqueness.

The distinction of *Cao Cao and Yang Xiu* from the other plays of the same time is also due to its open prospective in handling the subjects. Following the long period when plays were simply echoes of political ideology, what *Cao Cao and Yang Xiu* aims to achieve, is not illustrating political theory with historical stories, and not letting audience make awkward matches between history and reality, but a profound resonance that is universal in all the times.

If judged by the history of existence and the abundance of traditional resources, Huangmei Opera is not outstanding. It originated from Tea-Picking Tune in Huangmei County, Hubei. Huangmei County used to suffer constant droughts. Every time one came, a huge group of victims would move to Anqing, Anhui, where they made a living by singing. That was how the Tea-Picking Tune was widely popularized and finally developed into

Huangmei Opera in Anqing.

After the 1950s, owing to the wide spread of many classical plays such as *Fairy Couple and The Cowherd and the Weaving Girl* (*Niu Lang Zhi Nü*), the impact of Huangmei Opera quickly expanded. *Huizhou Woman* (*Hui Zhou Nü Ren*), a new play of Huangmei Opera acted by Han Zaifen in 1998, managed to bring great vitality to the style.

Huizhou Woman is a distinctive play. The heroine is a woman of no name living in a typical village of Huizhou. She gets married at the age of fifteen in hopes of beautiful and happy life. But her husband leaves the family on the wedding day because he refuses the arranged marriage and is eager for a new life. For 35 years, she stays with the family, desperately looking forward to her husband's return. Waiting becomes the only meaning in her life. She could have a new life of her own, but she chooses to wait, rather than walk away from the cage in her mind. Thirty-five years later, her husband returns, but he already has a new family. She is confused and wants to retreat, not knowing whether there is a way back.

The name of the heroine in *Huizhou Woman* is never mentioned. By presenting her without a name, her living environment and her lifestyle, it seems to doubt or question traditional Chinese ethics and morals, but also shows the heroine's comprehension of the significance of a woman's life from the prospective of an unknown woman. The uniqueness of *Huizhou Woman* also lies in the breakthroughs of its dramatic structure and stage arrangement, where there is no story, but only a presentation of a state of mind. The gestures and makeup of the heroine played by Han Zaifen though to a large extent abandon the aesthetic traditions of Huangmei Opera, yet are embodied with another kind of appealing effect. The use of bright colors and eclogue-styled aestheticism on stage, together with the visual effect of old houses of Anhui, created a natural relation between the fate of the figure and the cultural background she has been raised in. Therefore, her fate surpasses the level of her individual experience, becoming

Huizhou Woman, a new play of Huangmei Opera. Han Zaifen acts the leading role.

a metaphor of the fate of Chinese traditional women. While in the field of opera, the play clearly expresses the strong desire of Chinese Opera to synchronize with the world in stage arrangement and performance.

The Liyuan Opera *Mr. Dong and Mrs. Li* (*Dong Sheng Yu Li Shi*) reveals another important developing trend of Chinese Opera in the late of the 20th century. After experiencing long standing doubts and criticism to traditional culture, dramatists begin to review the permanent value of Chinese opera and cultural traditions. *Mr. Dong and Mrs. Li* is just a representative of that significant transformation.

Liyuan Opera originated from the Minnan dialect region in Fujian and Taiwan. Its representative plays, including *Gao Wenju, Chen San and Wu Niang*, have been passed to this day since the Song Dynasty. The present version of *Chen San and Wu Niang* is almost the same as the edition published in the 45th year of Jiajing Emperor of Ming Dynasty (1566), from which we could see its long history and astonishingly good preservation. Today's Liyuan Opera keeps the role system and its standard performing patterns from Song Yuan Nan Opera, requiring performers to strictly follow the aesthetic principles. Many musical patterns from the Tang and Song Dynasties are maintained. Similar to the times of the Tang Dynasty, the lutes are all horizontally played; the *erxian* are derived from *xiqin* in the Jin Dynasty; and the vertical flutes are actually *chiba* of Tang Dynasty. No other opera category today can compare with Liyuan Opera in its complete preservation of the performing pattern that has even utilized even before Ming Dynasty.

By generating new creations, *Mr. Dong and Mrs. Li* manages to represent the traditional pattern of Liyuan Opera, whose taste and rhyme are greatly appealing and delightful. The story is adapted from a modern novel, telling of an old landlord whose family name is Peng who doesn't trust his young wife with the family name of Li. Before he dies, he asks the family teacher Mr. Dong to supervise her. But Dong and Li fall in love and find their happiness.

A stage photo of Liyuan Opera *Mr. Dong and Mrs. Li.*

The playwright Wang Renjie knows very well the patterns of traditional poems and dramas. His work has pure figures, a simple structure, beautiful language and fresh style. More important, he has the most valuable cultural consciousness that makes him believe in the charm of traditional operas. The joint efforts of Su Yanshuo, director of the Quanzhou Liyuan Opera League, and Zeng Jingping and Gong Wanli, the main performers, help to bring the inherent elegance and delicacy further into perfection.

Mr. Dong and Mrs. Li provides a rare example: It fully reveals the creators' great respect for the historical and cultural value of local art. But in an environment full of communication and conflict of diverse cultures, the calm status of mind of the creators helps them integrate nationalism with modernism. Regardless of whether in creation or performance, *Mr. Dong and Mrs. Li* can be regarded as the peak in the field of traditional drama in modern China. It represents the highest level in drama creation and performance in modern times.

From the beginning of the 21st century, influenced by UNESCO's global selection of intangible cultural heritage, hundreds of traditional opera categories have been supported and specially protected by the central and local governments. More than one century earlier, dominated by the mighty western cultural values, whether intended or not, Chinese Opera in general tried to convert the oriental artistic tradition according to the dramatic theories introduced from the west. The trend has changed obviously since the beginning of the 21st century. Chinese Opera is on one hand further integrated with the world, while on the other returning to its traditions.

Intangible cultural heritage
In 1998, the United Nations Educational, Scientific and Cultural Organization (UNESCO) officially launched the project to protect representative oral and intangible cultural heritage. The aim is to set up an international award, which will be given to the most representative cultural spaces, or traditional and national cultural expressions. Inspired by that, rescue and protection of oral and intangible heritage in China has spread widely. As part of the intangible cultural heritage, many local opera categories, which are on the point of extinction, have now received more attention and protection.

Appendix:
Chronological Table of the Chinese Dynasties

The Paleolithic Period	Approx. 1,700,000–10,000 years ago
The Neolithic Age	Approx. 10,000–4,000 years ago
Xia Dynasty	2070–1600 BC
Shang Dynasty	1600–1046 BC
Western Zhou Dynasty	1046–771 BC
Spring and Autumn Period	770–476 BC
Warring States Period	475–221 BC
Qin Dynasty	221–206 BC
Western Han Dynasty	206 BC–AD 25
Eastern Han Dynasty	25–220
Three Kingdoms	220–280
Western Jin Dynasty	265–317
Eastern Jin Dynasty	317–420
Northern and Southern Dynasties	420–589
Sui Dynasty	581–618
Tang Dynasty	618–907
Five Dynasties	907–960
Northern Song Dynasty	960–1127
Southern Song Dynasty	1127–1279
Yuan Dynasty	1206–1368
Ming Dynasty	1368–1644
Qing Dynasty	1616–1911
Republic of China	1912–1949
People's Republic of China	Founded in 1949